UNFINISHED BUSINESS

True Accounts in

A Medium's Life as an Exorcist

UNFINISHED BUSINESS

True Accounts in
A Medium's Life as an Exorcist

BY

ELIZABETH BARON

Cover artwork by Elizabeth Baron

First published in 2000 by Random House, Inc., New York, New York.

Manufactured in the United States of America

ISBN: 0-75961-010-X

This book is printed on acid free paper.

1stBooks - rev. 3/7/01

Other Books, Videos and Audio tapes
by
Elizabeth Baron And Sandra Frazier-Delsignore

ASTRAL TRAVEL: A Spiritual Experience (audio)
COLOR THERAPY: Healing by Colors (audio)
Deep Relaxation (audio)
Dream Interpretation (audio)
EAT, DRINK AND THINK YOUR WAY TO A BETTER
    LIFE(audio)
FASTING-NATURE'S WAY OF HEALING(audio)
HEAL YOURSELF (audio)
KARMA AND REINCARNATION (audio)
HOW TO MEDITATE (audio)
Practical Vegetarianism (audio)
SELF ACCEPTANCE (audio)
STOP SMOKING (audio)

The Eating Habit (book)
THE ART OF SILENCE (book)
The Elizabeth Baron Special (video)
The Mystic Artist (book by Sandy Frazier-Delsignore)
Resurrection (CD by Sandy Frazier-Delsignore)

ACKNOWLEDGEMENTS

I would like to thank the following people:

My children who are my best friends. They have taken a lot of harassment and jokes tossed at them over the years for having a mother who is a medium, which made their life difficult.

Those people who have experienced the hauntings. Thank you for trusting me enough to invite me into your homes and allowing me to be the channel for your loved ones to come through to take care of their unfinished business.

All my friends who have joined me in these little excursions, doing the exorcisms: Howie, Jim, Glennis, and all those friends in New York City, especially Geri Palladino, who made the way for us to do the channeling at the great and famous theatres of Manhattan.

My guardian angel, St. Catherine of Siena, for always being there when we have called upon her spirit to come through and help us to understand the unknown so that we could get beyond our ignorance and go ahead with the exorcisms.

My daughter, Sandy, for all the inspiration and hard work she has given me over the years. Were it not for her, I would probably not be a medium at all. Thanks, Sandy, for believing in me, sometimes when I didn't believe in myself.

To Eileen Jones for writing a beautiful screenplay of my life; perhaps someday it will be a motion picture.

All those with whom I have experienced psychic phenomena, and are not individually acknowledged here.

Above all, I would like to thank The Source for giving me this wonderful gift of mediumship. Without it, I could never have had the wonderful, mystical experiences I have had my life showered with. I feel extremely lucky to have chosen to do this work. Anyone who definitely knows their purpose in life is very fortunate.

DEDICATION

I dedicate this book to my deceased loved ones: my mother and father, grandmother and grandfather; Theresa and Rudy Overstolz, my wonderful in-laws; my sisters, Ruth and Shirley Anne; my brothers Charles, Gene and Junior; and especially to my ex-husbands, Chief Warrant Officer Richard D. Frazier who served his country in Korea through the United States Army and Retired Chief of Police Robert Overstolz, who served his country in Korea through the United States Marine Corps. May God rest your souls and may you be at peace with Him forever and ever. It has been the pain that I suffered from losing you that spurred me on as a medium.

TABLE OF CONTENTS

PROLOGUE

Exorcism is the practice of expelling demons or spirits from persons, places, or things believed either to be possessed by them or to be in danger of possession. The rite is generally performed by a priest, shaman, or medicine man. Exorcism was commonplace in ancient times and at that time was based on magic. Babylonian priests, for example, would destroy a clay or wax image of the demon after reciting incantations. They believed that through this action, the demon itself would be destroyed. Similar rites were practiced by the Egyptians and Greeks. Belief in evil spirits and exorcism has survived in some American Indian and African religions as well.

In both the Old and New Testaments, the existence of devils and the efficacy of exorcism are presumed. The Gospels are filled with descriptive narratives about exorcisms performed by Jesus Christ. His method was not based on magic, however; rather he expelled evil spirits by prayer and by the power of his command. And he said, "This you too can do and even better than I, if you have the faith of a grain of mustard seed."

In both the Eastern and Western churches, rites of exorcism are still performed by the priest as part of the baptismal ritual, but other exorcisms are rare. Many Christians still believe in the devil but recognize that what was once believed to be possession can usually be treated as a psychological disorder. The Roman ritual contains an official rite of exorcism, but it can be used only with Episcopal permission.

The above is the description and information *Funk and Wagnall's New Encyclopedia* gives on exorcisms. This is the traditional belief that is held about exorcisms. However, there are many trance mediums across the world who are called on to do the rites of exorcism. Unfortunately, unless one is seeking this kind of service, these exorcists are rarely ever heard of. More popularly known are those mediums who use their gift in a sensational and entertaining way by selling their services of communicating with the dead. Today this is one of the most common ways mediums are using their talents.

Before I became an exorcist, I watched many mediums on television going through haunted houses, expressing to the audience that there were indeed ghosts in that particular building. However, they would stop right there.

Spirits and ghosts just don't hang around a building, home of a loved one, the place of their murder for nothing. Most ghosts appear to give the living warnings or sometimes they have lost their way at the time of death. Some are confused and lonely. Many of these spirits just need someone to talk with them and help them on their way. It does little good to make contact with a spirit unless the exorcist completes the job.

There is an unbelievable number of lost souls or spirits all over the world that need help in going on into the Light. Gettysburg is one of the most haunted places in America; these poor soldiers are still there waiting for someone to rescue them. The spirits of soldiers both Union and Confederate are stranded at strategic places all over the South on Sullivan's Island and all over the beaches of Charleston, South Carolina. The spirits of the Native Americans are there at Wounded Knee still running from the White Man in fear. My hope and dream is to one day be able to fund a tour in these haunted places where, as a medium and exorcist, I can be used by the Creator to help release these souls from their misery. It would be the greatest honor that I could have bestowed upon me.

Ever since the first exorcism I performed in 1980, I have always been very interested in wayward and earthbound spirits and decided to dedicate my life to helping these lost souls, as well as living souls, find their way into the Light. Therefore, I have written in this book my experience with thirty-four exorcisms, which I have conducted over the years. My purpose for writing this book is to help others to confirm their feelings about the reality of an afterlife and to offer non-believers the opportunity to look behind that big curtain beyond and at least consider expanding their awareness to consider that life goes on and on and on, even after dropping the physical body. With this book, I hope to shed a little light on this subject by sharing my own real life experiences.

— **Elizabeth Baron**
Charleston, South Carolina
May 13, 2000

FOREWORD

All my life I have wondered about the existence of life after death. I would hear about it during church sermons, see it in themes of motion pictures and television shows and read about it in books. The thought of what happens to us when we leave our bodies has always been a nagging one to me. That is, until I had the privilege of knowing Elizabeth Baron both professionally and as a very good friend. I have known Elizabeth since 1986.

Throughout the many years of a growing friendship with Elizabeth, I have witnessed inanimate objects shake and move, electronic devices turn on without batteries, and have even spoken to her guardian angel, St. Catherine of Siena, when Elizabeth went into full trance and brought her spirit through.

I even have been present on several of her exorcisms of houses and buildings that are described in this publication. However, I had only experienced seeing one vague apparition until Elizabeth and I were traveling back to Charleston from one of her media interviews in Atlanta, Georgia on December 22, 1994. The time was about 2:45 a.m. and it was raining so heavily on Interstate-26 that truck drivers had pulled over and filled the rest area parking spaces; leaving only the emergency lane for others to stop and wait out the storm. We were just outside St. George, South Carolina when I had slowed down to about thirty miles per hour for safety's sake. Elizabeth was just awakening from a short nap in the rear seat when we both saw a young woman simultaneously in the emergency lane. She was hitchhiking with her right arm extended as far out as it could go and her thumb out in a very enthusiastic manner. I found myself concentrating on her very big smile when I noticed some very peculiar things about her. She was wearing a blue-gray jogger's suit, but it was powder dry. There were just deep black holes where her eyes should be and she was floating at least a foot above the ground. I had slowed down even more and when we passed her, she disappeared.

I said to Elizabeth, "Did you see that?"

"Oh, yes, I did. It was a ghost," she responded.

Chills ran up my spine and my body shook in tremors for a long time afterward. We talked and discussed the event the rest of the way home. Several weeks later, a friend of the deceased girl came to see Elizabeth for a reading and Elizabeth was able to tell her of our experience. It turned out to be very meaningful and special for that person. She was the deceased's best friend. The Holy Spirit does indeed work in mysterious ways to give us messages from the afterlife.

Since that time, life after life (as I now refer to it) has taken on a very real and personal meaning for me. I no longer fear shedding my body and being taken into the Light for I know it is part of the Divine order of things. It is therefore my sincere hope that this book will be of help in answering similar questions that others may have.

— **JAMES R. SMYRE, M.ED., ED.S.**

"If some quiet night
You should hear a small whisper,
Answer quickly before a voice from
The Afterlife escapes you.
It just may be your lost love
Letting you know that all is not lost;
That the human soul nor love never dies".

— **Elizabeth Baron**

INTRODUCTION

WHAT IS AN EXORCISM?

In Webster's dictionary, the definition of <u>exorcism</u> is as follows: *the act of driving out evil spirits by commanding it, in the name of God, to depart, or by using incantations, charms etc to free a person or place from the possession of evil spirits.*

The definition of an <u>exorcist</u> is *someone who exorcises evil spirits; the second highest of the minor orders of the Roman Catholic Church.*

Exorcisms have been done by priests of the Catholic Churches for centuries; however, they have also been done by trance mediums such as myself for centuries. As a medium, I do not completely agree with the above definition in Webster's as it states that these are always "evil spirits."

On the contrary, I find that spirits who are "wayward" or "earthbound" as we call this state of being, are not evil at all but are just confused. The definition of <u>evil</u> in this same dictionary is *wicked, an evil man, evil counsels, arising from or caused by real or supposed wickedness, evil glean, disgusting, foul, disastrous, ill-omened, morally wrong.*

I do not say that evil spirits do not exist. However, I have found that most of the spirits of people I have been called on to exorcise are usually there to take care of "unfinished business" or sometimes to warn others of tragedies they are about to encounter; tragedies that they themselves may have suffered when they were living.

Drawing on the experiences I have had over the last twenty years as a trance medium and exorcist, I have found that those who die with unresolved issues, whether good or bad, will keep trying to reach their loved ones over and over until somehow, they make contact.

The only way the human soul can rest, after being taken by death, is to be one with God. That is why it is so necessary to believe in a Higher Being, a Creator of one's soul. Dwelling on the good in life; coming to terms with family and marital differences; seeing the good in oneself; forgiving everyone and worshipping the Creator helps one to have peace after death.

I have done life readings for many medical doctors and psychiatrists over the years. A number of them have told me that when one of their patients dies, they have seen a transparent object the size of a baseball go out of their solar plexus, arising up and away. I have been told by my guardian angel that this is one's soul going on to another place, another dimension. This is the part of us that never dies. Our soul is eternal.

If a father has been fighting with his son just before death, he will continue to try and resolve that fight in his death state. There are many dimensions in the universe. In each of those dimensions, there is a learning state of consciousness. When death first takes our life, we go to a place the Catholics call Purgatory. This is a stopping-off place, where our lives are played back to us and we are able to see the mistakes we made on earth. Our job is to make amends for those mistakes in many ways.

First, if we killed another while on earth, we may reincarnate as that person's wife or husband and stay with that person till death do we part. We literally owe our life to that individual. If we were very good to another person in the last lifetime, perhaps we will return to that person's life and be a husband or wife or best friend to that individual, living a life of happiness. That debt we owe, good or bad, is called karma. The process of returning to another body in a future life is called reincarnation.

However, before we can go on to another life, sometimes it is necessary to take care of the karma we have created here on earth. Therefore we will keep trying and trying to communicate with our loved ones so that we can make up for the wrongs we have done. The soul does not rest until we have taken care of that unfinished business.

The following chapters are true stories; only the names have been changed to protect the individuals' privacy. These chapters will show the reader just how all this phenomenon plays out in different people's lives.

WHERE DOES THE SOUL GO WHEN SOMEONE DIES?

In 1978 I had a reading from a wonderful medium/minister named David in California. He was visiting a church in San Diego, where he preached sermons and did readings. He said to me in the reading, "You have been asking God where the soul goes when it dies." I was shocked! No one knew that except myself and God. Then he continued, "You have checked out two books from the library. Both are navy blue, one has a plastic cover and one is cloth. Look in the one that is cloth covered on pages 17 through 27 and you will have your answer."

I could hardly wait to get to my home where the books were laid out on my bed. Sure enough, when I opened the cloth-covered book called *Genuine Mediumship*, there was the answer. I cannot quote because I don't have the book anymore but it went like this,

> When a person dies, the soul lives on. However, it doesn't go anywhere. There are a thousand dimensions where you sit — a thousand worlds. The soul, when it leaves the body, just goes into one of those dimensions.

I felt because of the way this information came to me that it was Truth and I have held onto that Truth since that time.

One of these dimensions the soul can go into is here on earth. If a person is dying and he does not want to die, sometimes it is possible for him to immediately go into another person's body, especially a sick child or someone who does not protect himself from "psychic intrusion." When this happens, it is called transmigration of souls. We will show you an example of this process in another chapter. This process is listed in Webster's Dictionary and was fully explained to us by my guardian angel, Catherine of Siena. I was not familiar with this at all until we had to deal with it in an exorcism.

I would recommend baptizing your baby, especially if you are caring for an elderly father or mother or loved one in your home while the child is young. The child has a right to live her own life and should be afforded this right by the parents who are naturally interested in her psychological health. The rite of Baptism can afford spiritual protection for the child.

MY INTRODUCTION TO THE "OTHER WORLD"

In 1978, I had a horrible experience in Chicago, Illinois — my home since I was a young girl. I was beaten severely and was hospitalized for awhile, suffering from a brain concussion and a skull fracture. I had just gone through a horrible divorce and was really suffering from depression over the loss of my husband.

At that time, I had a spiritual experience, something I call, "an encounter with God." Because of my sadness and feeling of helplessness, I cried out to my Creator. Suddenly, a masculine Presence came to me in a bright light. He took me upon a mountain in a vision-like way. "My child, it is time to do your work." He explained to me that he had a mission for me to do and he showed me a small garden of roses. "These pink roses represent my children. If you will treat them kindly, look what I have for you in the future." He then showed me roses as far as I could see. He also told me He would send me one of his special angels to help me.

A few weeks later, he sent the spirit of a nun. She appeared in a bright light in my room one cold February morning in Chicago. She spoke not a word but walked straight into my body. She is still with me today. Her name is St. Catherine of Siena, a fourteenth century nun. She was one of two women ever given the title of "doctor" in the Catholic Church. Bear in mind, I was not a Catholic. I had been brought up as a devout Baptist and we were taught to defy the teachings about the

Virgin Mother, which was the real difference between our beliefs.

About a year after Catherine came to me, I did my first exorcism as is recorded in Chapter 2. At that time, I never dreamed I would ever be doing exorcisms and I had never connected my psychic "gift" with any such thing.

Chapter 1

MY FIRST ENCOUNTER WITH A GHOST

Shortly after the spirit of St. Catherine came to me in Chicago, I moved to San Diego, California to work on my spiritual pathway. I went to a Spiritualist Church on 42nd Street and worked on my mediumship. This was a small white wooden church, very simple in a simple part of town but the members were all young to middle age people and most of them were very sincere. This church was made up mostly of people who were trying to develop their psychic ability... mediums, psychics, and healers.

One afternoon while sitting up on my bed in a private room I had rented, I was reading a book. Suddenly the ghost of a young man I had known in Chicago appeared in my doorway. John had been murdered in an elevator of a Chicago business office building a few years before. It was alleged that his murder was done by the Chicago Mafia; it was also alleged that they were trying to get John's brother-in-law for starting a burglar alarm company in competition with theirs. His body was solid and he looked just like he had always appeared when I knew him with the exception of his eyes... they were missing. Instead, there was nothing but black holes where his beautiful blue eyes had once appeared.

I was very frightened and began to surround myself with the White Protective Light of God (which I had learned to do at the Spiritualist Church in California.) I was taught to protect myself from any negative spirits who might be around me or I was to learn later, from the negative side of <u>me</u>.

"Ah, you didn't do that when I was living," he said through a type of mental telepathy I had become familiar with through my other experiences with the Creator and the spirit of St. Catherine.

"I know," I answered. "But, I am afraid of you now that you are dead," I told him.

"Well, you don't have to be; I just want you to do me a favor... when you return to Chicago in August, I want you to go to my wife and tell her that I was not responsible for my death. Tell her they were after her brother. I just got in the line of fire; in other words I was guilty by association," he pleaded.

"I can't do that, and besides, I'm not going back to Chicago for a long time. I like it here in San Diego and I'm going to stay here till I feel better about myself," I spoke to him in the haughty way I had talked with him when he was alive.

"You <u>are</u> going back for a little while in August and I would appreciate it if you would call my wife and give her the message I gave to you."

"How do you know I'm going back in August? I haven't planned a trip back to Chicago," I answered him.

"Trust me, you will go back in August; just do what I ask," and then he disappeared!

I promised myself that if I did go back to Chicago and found it easy to get John's wife's telephone number, I would call her. But if I had to really work to find it, I would not bother.

In August, just before my birthday, Cutty and Diane, two of the friends I had made since moving to San Diego, gave me a gift. I was so surprised when I opened it and there was an airplane ticket to travel to their wedding in New York. On the return ticket, they had made arrangements for me to stop at my home in Chicago for a few days' visit and then return to San Diego. I still get chills when I think of this experience. This whole ghost business was very new to me and was sometimes hard to swallow. I could certainly understand those who have never had a personal ghostly experience... why they are such skeptics. But here was living proof. John had told me I would go back in August and now I would be on my way.

When I returned to Chicago, I went to my daughter, Sandy's apartment to visit. It was so beautiful in Chicago. August is hot there, but the flowers are blooming and the trees are all green — just a prelude to autumn when the trees begin to change color and the threat of the cold winds begin to surface. I arrived at

O'Hare Airport late in the evening. Sandy was waiting for me at the airport. It was so good to see her. She and I are not only mother and daughter, but have always been able to inspire each other. We are both artists along with our other business interests; so when we get together it is something to behold. And we never leave each other without doing a quick watercolor painting together.

The first thing I did was to go to Sandy's bedroom and call John's place of business where he worked before he was murdered.

"Yes", the lady answered. "We still have his family's phone number." "How ironic!" I thought to myself.

I immediately called his wife. I told her what her dead husband, John had told me. His phone number had been so easy to attain that I knew I was doing the right thing.

"Thank you so much for the information. You know, his mother is Catholic. She baby-sits with the children quite often. We have a tree in our living room that shakes every time she comes over. She swears it is John trying to communicate. Elizabeth, she will be so thrilled to hear from her son and I do thank you from the bottom of my heart for calling."

I was so pleased! I had delivered my first message from the dead to evidently clear up the "unfinished business" John's ghost had wanted so to do.

It would be years before I would see the spirit of John again. However, three years later I saw the shadow of his face in my windshield. I asked him what he wanted. He begged me to contact his wife because one of his sons was very ill.

I guess I wasn't very compassionate at that time and so I said, "Please go away, I can't do anything about your son being ill! I've lost your wife's phone number and even if I did call her, it wouldn't make a lot of difference; I mean, there's nothing you or I can do."

He disappeared so fast and I never saw him again. I felt really bad about the fact that I didn't try to help contact his wife again. I still do. At the time, I guess I was caught up in my own problems and a part of my ego was getting quite large as I was fastly becoming well known as a medium.

Chapter 2

THE GHOST OF BOBBY SAVES FAMILY'S LIVES

In December of 1978, I had returned from San Diego to my home in Chicago. At first I took a job working as an assistant to the President of a small management consultant firm. However, it was just a short time before I was working as a full time trance medium, giving readings to numerous people from all walks of life. At this time, I had never connected my gift at all with exorcisms and certainly did not know I was capable of even being involved in such a process.

I was quite surprised in December of 1979 when my son, John, came to me and asked if I would go to his girlfriend, Lori's home in Elgin, Illinois — a far northwest suburb of Chicago — and do an exorcism for her family. At the time, my children and I were living in Schaumburg, Illinois a western suburb of Chicago. It was December, one of the coldest months in Chicago. I felt extremely insufficient and unqualified to do this kind of work. As a matter of fact, it almost frightened me to even think of doing something like this.

"Why in the world would you think that I would be able to do an exorcism?" I had asked my son.

"Well," he said, "you have seen ghosts and you can talk to your guardian angel, who is dead. Why can't you help these ghosts get out of Lori's house?"

"What is happening up there, Johnny?" I asked purely out of curiosity.

"Wow, Mom, all sorts of things! Lori's father was sitting in the living room watching television and all of a sudden, the Christmas tree started swinging back and forth. The little area rug under his feet started flying across the room and landed in the baby's playpen. The baby started standing on its hands and the dog began to stand on its front legs," he explained excitedly.

"Please, please, would you go up there with us? Just try!" he begged.

My first impression of this whole thing was that I was, in fact, at a standstill. I honestly did not know what to do. So I called a priest and asked him if he would go to the home of these people and do this exorcism.

"Are they Catholic?" he asked.

"What difference does that make?" I asked him.

"Well, the rule in our church is that we do exorcisms for our members but we do not provide this service for non-members," he explained.

"But, Father, these people need you. Maybe if you go and do this exorcism and get rid of these spirits, they will become members of your church," I begged.

"I'm sorry! I have to abide by the church's rules. Besides all priests are not exorcists and I am surely not one of those highly qualified holy men of the Catholic Church. I don't make the rules. They make these rules at the Vatican," he said sadly.

"How sad! I guess I'm going to have to go and try to do this myself," I almost raised my voice in anger. I wasn't happy at all that he would not come with me. I realized at that moment that there was a need for exorcists who would go to any person in need of an exorcism, regardless of their race or religion. And although I certainly did not know how to go about doing this ritual, I knew that I had my guardian angel who would help me in any way she could. After all she was the spirit of a Catholic nun who had been recognized by the church in such high esteem that they had declared her not only a saint but also had given her the title of doctor, which means teacher in the Catholic Church... as a matter of fact, this title had only been bestowed upon one other nun in the Catholic Church and that was Teresa of Avila. I felt I couldn't be in better hands. Catherine was highly qualified to do an exorcism and later, I found that she did do exorcisms in the fourteenth century. I would allow her to use my body, mind, and spirit to do so again.

I finally told Johnny that I would go to Lori's house and see what I could do. The weather was horrible in Chicago at that time of year. It was about ten degrees outside. Having been born in the South, I never ever got use to the cold weather in the North, although I lived there for many years. I put on the warmest clothes I could find along with my winter boots and a beautiful red scarf I wore to complement my dark hair. I looked in the mirror and saw myself aging. I was already into my late thirties and at that time, I could not imagine giving up any of my life to do exorcisms. At that time, I also did not in my wildest dreams, understand the commitment and self-discipline that came with being an exorcist.

Priests take vows of celibacy, poverty, chastity and obedience. They are committed to pray, meditate and to live a life as a role model to others. No way was I committed to any of these goals at that time. It would be years before I was willing to commit to anything except myself. However, I would pray and ask the Creator to help me to help these people — Johnny's friend and her family.

I'd like to mention that priests in general are not exorcists. The ones who are chosen to do exorcisms are very well disciplined and live "by the rules of the church." I recall a movie called, *The Exorcist,* which was based on a true story. The young priest who was assisting the old priest, died by being so possessed of guilt... guilt that he carried with him day in and day out over the fact that his mother was in a nursing home. This was a situation he could do nothing about because he had taken a vow of poverty as a priest, even though he was trained as a psychiatrist and could have been making a lot of money and therefore would have been able to take care of his mother financially. So even though he was a priest and a good one, he died by allowing the demon to possess him so with guilt that he jumped out the window to his death.

On this cold night in December of 1979, Johnny, my son and I traveled about twenty-five miles northwest to Elgin, a very small suburb where many traditional people lived. The houses were beautifully lined up on the street with all the colorful Christmas decorations. To observe the neighborhood as we drove down this beautiful street of Victorian homes, one would never think that turmoil and mystery would lurk behind the doors of any of these places. As we came to the door of Lori's home, her parents both answered the doorbell, looking so frightened.

"Please come in!" they both said, enthusiastically, at the same time. Johnny and I both were protected with very warm clothing; however, we experienced just as much cold air after entering their house as we did outside. Their home was decorated in a lovely and cozy way, yet there was an air of strangeness throughout the area.

Lori's father sat down in his favorite chair and started explaining how, just before we came, the small throw rug under his feet had flown across the room and landed in the baby's playpen. As he was explaining the phenomena, I looked over toward the Christmas tree. I could not believe what I saw! The Christmas tree was going back and forth as if something was pushing on it. And even though it was moving, all the ornaments were not shaken off. We then went to the dining room and there was a small horse attached to the light in the ceiling. This horse was going round and round as if it were mechanically affected.

They took us to the master bedroom and showed us how the bed raised about two feet off the floor when the parents were sleeping. It would then begin to rock. They showed us a small room upstairs, which seemed especially cold to me and I felt somehow that this was the space the ghost occupied.

We all returned to the living room where a lot of the activity was going on. I asked for a comfortable chair to sit on. Lori brought me a wooden straight back chair from the kitchen and placed it in the middle of the living room. I sat there and prayed that I would be led to do this exorcism properly, even though I had never done one in my life. I somehow knew that the Holy Spirit would lead me to do the right thing. After all, I was possessed by my nun, St. Catherine of Siena, one of the greatest exorcists of the 14th Century.

After the prayer,

"Thank you Father for allowing me to serve you. Please lead me to allow your servant, St. Catherine to take over and do this exorcism using my body, mind and spirit. In the name of the Father, the Son, and the Holy Ghost, I pray,"

I somehow seemed to know the procedures. I asked Lori's mother to get me a Bible and I set it on my lap. Now, I carry my own white St. Jerome's Bible, which was given me by a priest who became close to me while he was taking my meditation classes. This was a Holy Book I respect very much and so therefore, I believed its vibrations would give me some protection. I prayed for protection from any evil or negativity that might be in the house and surrounded myself with the Pure White Light of God.

Suddenly I began channeling the message that was given to me by Spirit: "There is a little fourteen-year-old boy named Bobby who is coming through and saying that there is danger here. He was burned twenty-five years ago in this house and he is telling us the house will burn again. 'Please get out of here by the end of February,'" he begged.

Then I went all over the house and asked God to bless and spiritually clean each room. I went into the corners of each and every room and allowed the Love of God to come through and purify the house. Everyone seemed to feel better. I thanked Bobby, the ghost, for coming to us and assured him that the family would be out by the end of February. Everything seemed to be okay when I left.

However, about a week later, Lori's father called me and said the spiritual disturbance had started again. I asked him what had changed to bring the ghost back. After talking with him, it seemed that the family members had changed their minds about moving. Since the phenomena had stopped, they indeed had decided to stay. This was not agreeable with Bobby, the ghost.

He had come to warn them of the inevitable. I told him I could not come to Elgin right at that time. I wasn't feeling well and I wasn't sure I had the ability to be an exorcist. I asked them to call a group called the "Ghostbusters"; these people went around to haunted houses and tried to remove spirits all the time. They had become very popular among the psychic community in Chicago. I seriously thought that maybe they could help this troubled family.

Shortly thereafter, I received another call from Lori's father. "Elizabeth, the Ghostbusters are up here and they are saying you are crazy; they say there's nothing in the house, especially no young boy named Bobby."

"Okay, I answered, "do you know anyone in the neighborhood who knows the history of the house?"

"Yes, as a matter of fact, the man across the street built the house," he remarked.

"Would you please go over and ask him if he knows of a young boy named Bobby who lived there and if the house has ever burned?"

"I will call you right back, Elizabeth," he said and hung up the phone. I eagerly awaited an answer.

About an hour later he called me, laughing profusely! "Elizabeth, the man across the street told me that there was indeed a young boy named Bobby who burned to death in the room upstairs... you know, the one in which you felt so strange! He said that was about twenty-five years ago. When I told the Ghostbusters, they couldn't get out of here fast enough! You should have seen them, Elizabeth! They were scared out of their minds. Now will you come up here?" he pleaded.

I was elated! I was shouting with joy! I really, really had made contact!

I finally went to the house in Elgin for the second time and talked with Bobby. We made a promise to him that the family would be out of the house before the end of February. I asked him not to bother the family anymore. We also let him know how much we appreciated this warning. I asked the Father to take him on into the Light where he could continue his work on his own spiritual path. He began to see the "Light" and followed it!

I had a small meditation group by that time so I had taken them with me. We all took white candles... white represents purity and sincerity. Some of the group were frightened of the haunted house but were eager to participate in an exorcism of the phenomena. When we left, everything and everybody was at peace.

Just before the end of February of 1980, the family had packed all their belongings into a rented truck with plans of moving to Florida. They went to a restaurant to have some breakfast before starting their long ride. When they returned, a fire had started which burned part of the house and part of the furniture in the truck. They fled to Florida, never wanting to see that house again. At the time, they begged me to write a story about this haunting, but at the time, I was so inexperienced at all this that I refused. I had no idea how to even begin to explain to others what really happened. I was so in awe that I had actually been a part of something so strange!

Chapter 3

A CHARLESTON HAUNTING

In June of 1980, I moved to Myrtle Beach, South Carolina. This city is one of the biggest tourist attractions on the East Coast where millions of families visit each year to allow their children to play on the beautiful beaches of the Atlantic Ocean. Shortly thereafter, I moved down the coast to one of the loveliest towns in the world, Charleston, South Carolina. Still living on the coast, this town is much more cultural and suitable for raising children. Its history is phenomenal. There are cannons in the downtown park right near the ocean at a place called the Battery. These cannons were used in the Civil War. The natives who have lived here all their lives are very proud of their heritage. There are also lovely old antebellum homes, which have been restored and are now fit for any King or Queen to reside in. There is so much history here that they make a business out of telling the tourists the stories of long ago. And tourism is one of the main businesses here.

I began doing psychic readings, television and radio shows and was swiftly building a good reputation as a trance medium. One night I was invited downtown Charleston to one of the big old Victorian homes by some friends I had met. I really can't even remember their names now because as soon as I came to Charleston, everyone was inviting me to their homes. I was somewhat of a phenomenon myself; being able to see the dead and feel the ghosts of the past; the people I met were fascinated with it all. That included me.

We were having a very nice dinner in this huge old house that reeked of the past. I would never want to live in any downtown Charleston house. I would never be able to sleep because of the many vibrations that have been left by dead families and their various problems they had while here on earth. These are the same problems which are passed on to their descendents without them even being aware of how much their ancestors are affecting their personal lives.

As we were having our dinner, suddenly the spirit of a woman in a long dress, which appeared to be of the late eighteen hundreds or early nineteen hundreds, appeared to me and began chitchatting. She told us how she had remained an old maid because she was in love with a married man and she wanted to be with him regardless of the circumstances. She told me that in those days one was not allowed to do so many things for fear of ridicule by the church and being tossed out of one's church and then continuously tortured by a horrible reputation.

The family I was visiting did not have the ability to see this woman; however, I mentioned the fact that I was conversing with her to them. They became really excited and knew exactly whom I was talking about.

"My, my, we always wondered why Aunt Ashley never married. So she was doing a little hanky panky, huh?" They laughed and laughed. They thought it was really brave of her to do something like that in those early times.

"I can send her into the Light of God, if you wish," I suggested to them. "She is lost in this house and has not been able to tear her soul away from here. This is not good. When you have a haunting in your house, it is your duty to ask that ghost to leave and go on to the Light. Otherwise, her misery and anxiousness will affect your lives."

"No, no, no, we can't let you get rid of our ghost. It is our ghost and we love living here with our ancestors still here," they said, to my amazement.

"But don't you realize that she is not in the Light, that she doesn't belong here? This is your house now and you have no privacy with your aunt here also," I begged.

"Never mind, Elizabeth, we like the fact that she is here."

"But she is a human being; you can't own her. She belongs with God!" I explained. However, shortly thereafter, I stopped trying to convince them, realizing that these people did not understand the afterlife and how ghosts could affect one's life if they were not asked to leave. In time to come, I would learn that many of the people of Charleston who lived in these old homes made part of their living by having tourists take "ghost walks" with them. They made money as a result of these phenomena. Why in the world would they want to get rid of their ghosts? There were churches full of ghosts; there were graveyards full of ghosts. There were beaches full of the ghosts of dead soldiers from the Civil War who still didn't know they had died and were still trying to find their way back to the Light, trying to find their pathway to God... Union soldiers as well as Confederate ones.

There was so much to experience in years to come. I was shocked and amazed at the gift I had been given to work with. I was in awe every time I had another experience with the afterlife and was so humble before God that I had been allowed this most wonderful privilege.

Chapter 4

EXORCISING A CIVIL WAR HOSPITAL

From 1980 to 1986, I traveled frequently around the southeast from state to state, attempting to build my reputation as a trance medium. I did television talk shows in each of these places I visited and did life readings for clients I met. At that time, I had no idea that I could do a life reading on the phone as well as in person, so I felt I had to go to the client or they had to come and visit me in my office in Charleston.

I remained with this ignorance until one of my clients moved to California and called me for a reading. She told me she wanted a reading on the phone. Of course, I explained to her that I could not do that... I felt she had to be present for me to touch and see her.

"Elizabeth, many mediums out here do readings on the phone. Try it... just tune into my vibrations and pretend I am there in front of you," she said anxiously. I did what she asked and from that time on, expanded my ability to communicate with clients across the world. Also, I did not have to travel anymore to do my job.

I had visited a place called Highpoint, North Carolina. One day I received a call from a young lady I had read for there on my last visit. Actually I had read for her and her boyfriend. I will call her Beth. Beth told me that she and her boyfriend had moved into an old, old house that had been there since the Civil War.

"What is happening up there Beth?" I asked her.

"Oh Elizabeth, we have been to psychiatrists, psychologists, doctors and no one could help us. Finally, a psychologist who had met you on one of your visits here told us to call you," she said. "We are about to go crazy! The toilet stops up constantly. We go to the bathroom and flush the commode and ten minutes later all this foul matter is coming up, and running over into the bathroom floor. We have had plumbers and they can find nothing wrong with the commode. My little boy who is eight years old is going around screaming that someone had to cut his hand off and he begged me to tie a white piece of cloth around it. He hurts so badly that he wants to jump out the window. This is causing so many problems between my boyfriend and myself. We can't sleep at night at all. Please help us!" she cried.

"I can't come up there right now; however I will be glad to speak with you and do what I can on the phone now. First, I would have the owner of the place level the building and build a brand new house. I can feel so much violence there. I believe that wounded soldiers have been there in the Civil War and the violence and pain is just too much. The vibrations of long ago are affecting your life and the life of your child. I ask you and your friend to pray for these souls who are still haunting the place and help them with perhaps a minister assisting them to go into the Light. However, because of the enormity of the pain there, I would move out of the place. These are my suggestions to you. Your young son is being possessed by that pain and by the ghosts of the house even as we speak. He's too young to fight them off. Please do as I ask and get your family out of there as soon as possible. Then go to the owner and ask him to not allow other people to experience what you have had to go through."

I understood from other phone conversations that they did indeed move and all was well with their family. I was also told that the building was burned down shortly thereafter. They called me a few months later to thank me for helping them with a problem no one seemed to be able to solve. At that time, they also said that they had done some investigation of the home and found that indeed, it had been a temporary hospital for wounded soldiers of the Civil War.

Chapter 5

GHOST OF 1821 SEEKS REVENGE

One day I was working at my office giving life readings when I received a call from a downtown Charleston businessman. He sounded really disturbed.

"Elizabeth, I really need you to come down to my home. I know there are ghosts in this house and I can't seem to sleep at night. My father has recently died and left this home to me. I am getting ready to be married to a wonderful woman but I can't bring her in this house when I know the place is haunted. Can you please help me?" he begged.

"Yes, I'll be down there in about an hour. I have one more client to take care of here in my office and then I'll drive to your home," I told him. My daughter Tami was about eight years old and for the first time, I took her with me because on such a short notice, I could not find a babysitter.

As we drove up to this beautiful mansion, I could hardly believe my eyes. The place had been recently remodeled and stood there as a stately reminder of bygone days. Its beautiful white porches with all the fine outdoor furniture just reminded me of long ago when the beautiful southern ladies with their long dresses sat there with their mint juleps and on occasion, bringing their fine white linen handkerchiefs out to properly and daintily wipe the corners of their mouths.

I stopped the car for a moment and just sat there; almost stunned as I visualized for a moment what it would be like to have lived there in the early 1800s. It would be grand to see the men in their fine silks and woolens, walking up one side of the stairway to the veranda while the women walked up the other side. I wondered what these people did for entertainment in those days, since television and radio had not been invented yet.

Momentarily, Tami and I got out of the car and began to walk up to the mansion. Soon we were ringing the doorbell and this gracious man, Steven, who was probably a reincarnation of the original owner, came to welcome us into the beautiful foyer. I stopped again and listened to the vibrations of long ago and it seemed that I could hear music and an orchestra playing as the men and women danced across the gorgeous area before me. The chandeliers were enormous and there was a beautiful winding stairway begging us to climb up to another part of the home.

Upon entering this beautiful mansion, I sensed the chilly feeling that can be defined by an exorcist as the first sign of a haunting. The house was grand in every way, but the vibrations cried out for someone to come and give that warm, cozy feeling. The young client explained to me that the house was over two hundred years old. It had been in his family in some way all that time.

I asked him to take me up to the top floor. I was following the vibrations like a police dog follows his senses to the source. When we got to the third floor, I knew I had found the home of the ghost. It was nearly freezing although the heat was on in every room of the house. I asked the client to take my little daughter Tami, back down to the first floor and watch her till I finished my work.

Before I could say anything else, Tami began to beg, "Mommy, I want that! I want that!"

"What?" I asked her.

"I want that tiger's head," she said, as she directed my attention towards an enormous bedroom with a big tiger rug and a tiger's head on the floor in front of the bed.

"Oh, honey, you can't have that. This tiger's head belongs to Mr. Jones," I pleaded with her.

"Oh no that's alright, she can have the whole thing," he said as he picked up the tiger rug with the head attached and handed it to Tami.

She was so thrilled! "Now, I'm the only kid in the neighborhood with a tiger's head," she bragged. She still has the tiger's head in her living room and is still very proud of it.

"Say thank you to the gentleman, Tami," I persuaded.

"Thank you! Oh, thank you!" she shouted with delight, as she headed down the stairs with my client.

I stood in front of the window in this huge bedroom, which was furnished with nineteenth-century furniture, everything in it having been handpicked in the earlier days. Perhaps this part of the house had not been occupied for many years, although with an unmade bed and things sort of flung around the rooms, it appeared that someone was presently living in the whole upstairs area. As soon as I stepped up to the window, the spirit of a young man flowed through me. He started mumbling as if talking to someone else.

"It is now 1821 and I hate my cousin across the street. He has been sleeping with my wife and I hate him for it," he complained. "I'll get him for it; I don't know how, but I'll get him. Look at him down there! He thinks no one knows what a scoundrel he is but I know!" he kept talking with enormous anger coming through.

I stepped away from the window and it seemed that he slipped out of my body at the same time. I knelt and prayed to God that He would remove this troubled spirit from this house and that He would send him on into His Holy Light.

I walked down the long stairway and as I got closer and closer to the bottom of the stairs where I met my daughter and my client, Steven Jones, I could feel the depression of the remembrance of those years long ago... leaving, slowly and gently flowing out of the mansion.

It was sometime afterward that this client sold his home and felt relieved of the burden he carried with the responsibility of having such a place, the responsibility of karma; karma from a time he would not consciously remember. However, I do believe this client was very deeply involved in this whole scenario many years ago... back in 1821, having built up karma he would have to rid himself of in this lifetime or go into life hereafter, only to come back and do it all over again.

Chapter 6

EXORCISM ON CHANNEL 2 - Six O'clock News

In late September of 1986, a friend of mine, Ted Knight, a news advocate for Channel 2 Television in Charleston, came and asked me if I would have lunch with him.

"Ted, I know you want me to do something for you or you wouldn't be asking me out to lunch," I laughed. Ted and I had known each other for a long time and we were always trying to make each other laugh. There was nothing more that Ted loved than the field of psychic phenomena. Once he brought the FBI to my office along with the Charleston County Sheriff's police to find an escaped "death row" convict who they had brought down from the prison in Columbia, South Carolina to appeal his case. He escaped from the cops and could not be found.

I remember saying to the FBI agent who Ted called *Ed the Fed*, "You always want me to help you but you never tell me whether the information helps," I said with resentment.

The Agent then spoke up: "If the information didn't help do you think the police would keep coming back to you? But if it makes you feel better, I asked one of the cops you were working with once if you could help locate a man who had killed his wife and buried her body on Edisto Beach, South Carolina. You told him you saw him in an orange truck in Toledo, Ohio heading down the main highway toward Florida. We picked him up in about four hours using your information. Now, does that make you feel better?" he asked as he smiled at me with approval.

Ted and I went to Athens Restaurant, a Greek restaurant not too far from my office. When we arrived there and sat down across from each other, he finally told me what he wanted me to do for him.

"Well, Elizabeth, to be very honest, I want you to do an exorcism on a house for the six o'clock news tonight."

"Tonight?" I shouted. I haven't had time to prepare for any exorcism. I have to fast and pray and do a three-day cleansing of body, mind and spirit. Do you want me to become possessed?"

"Oh, come on, Elizabeth, we don't have that kind of time. We must do it tonight."

"Who ever heard of doing an exorcism on the six o'clock news anyway?" I asked him.

"You know how much I admire your work, Elizabeth, do it for me," he begged.

"This woman called me today and is really scared. She has a ghost in her house. Please, can I count on you?"

"Well, I don't think I could pass this one up. I will come with you," I agreed.

Then he rushed me through my dinner so that we could get to the house and get the exorcism done. He would have to hurry back to the television station to be able to edit the film properly in time for the six o'clock news.

We drove to the little town of Mt. Pleasant, South Carolina, then to a small brick home, which appeared to have been built in the sixties. It was very modest on the outside. A nice friendly golden retriever met us at the door and seemed to be harmless. This appeared to be an average home in an average neighborhood... that is, until we got inside.

We rang the doorbell and were greeted by a very nice couple. They invited us into the living room and as soon as I sat down I noticed a sculpture of an Egyptian scarab on the wall along with photographs of the pyramids.

"Are you into Egyptology?" I asked.

"As a matter of fact, my husband is an Egyptologist," the young woman replied.

The husband chimed in, "We have spent much time in Egypt."

"Can you show me where you saw the apparition?" I asked. Susan, the young woman, led me into the kitchen and pointed to a corner by the sink.

"Right there," she said. "I can't believe this all happened! It seems like a bad dream."

"I was just standing there by the sink a few weeks ago, washing the dishes. I emptied the dishwater and left the kitchen because I had to go to the bathroom. When I came back, much to my amazement, the kitchen sink had been cleaned with the Comet that was setting on the sink and the floor had been completely mopped. The mop was standing on its end, straight up without any support and the apparition was in the corner. It was a man, I believe. I could see that it was a tall misty gray form and I could make out the men's shoes on the floor. It just stood there for a moment and then went away. The dog has been afraid to come back into the house. I had to go to Atlanta to stay with my mother for a few days because I was too afraid to stay here, even with my husband," she finished.

"Okay, let's go back into the living room and find a chair that I can sit in. I will then attempt to make contact with the apparition; when I leave, you will feel so much better," I explained to the young couple.

As soon as we gathered in the living room and I was quite comfortable in a wonderful overstuffed chair, I took a few deep breaths, asked for protection, said my prayers and then went into my usual trance.

"There is a man who was troubled when he was here on earth. He is a relative of yours. He had a wife but he didn't get along with her well. He is here in your home to tell you that he owes you an apology. Susan, he says to you that he's very sorry for the way he treated you when he was alive. He will stay around for about six months until you have gotten some help, maybe some therapy, so that you will be able to forgive him and then he will go on into the Light. He also wants you to find a place of worship that you can go to each Sunday," I kept conveying his messages to her.

The tears streamed down Susan's face and her husband comforted her with a hug, caressing her hand and putting his arms around her, holding her close. Ted was shocked; even though he believed in psychic phenomena and especially in my ability. He was always in awe of these kinds of gifts and wanted them so for himself. He began to ask Susan if the information meant anything to her.

"It sure does, it is my grandfather. I didn't go to his funeral last summer because I hated him for the way he treated me. I just couldn't forgive him for some of the personal things he did to me. He was always doing the dishes and mopping the kitchen floor for my grandmother. He loved to do the mopping! And now he has come here and mopped my floor. She cried some more. I should have recognized him immediately when he mopped my floor. Our whole family has always talked about him mopping," she cried, tears streaming down her face.

The husband spoke, "I want to thank you so much for coming here, because this means a lot to not only Susan and me but to our dog, Kali. She was afraid to come into the house but now she will be able to come back in. Susan and I will work on this forgiveness. I can see it has helped her. Thanks so much!"

Ted Knight spoke into the camera, "Well, I'm not going to comment on this but I will ask you Susan, why in the world did you call Action Line to take care of something like this?"

"Well, you said on television if you had a problem just call Ted Knight and that's what I did!" she said laughingly.

We said goodbye to two happy people and went home to watch the first exorcism in Charleston recorded on the six o'clock news.

In the years to come, Ted Knight would quit his job and move to New Mexico where he lived only a short time before he died of cancer. He called me a number of times to say hello and to let me know of his condition. He developed a fatal type of cancer.

About a year later he died. It was sometime later when one of his friends called me and told me his spirit was visiting her house. This let us know that he was alright, that he had made it over to the other side. I asked her to pray for him to go on into the Light. He had done his work down here on earth and he certainly needed to be in the Light of God.

Before he left South Carolina, he made me a beautiful ceramic vase and painted a winter scene on one side and a summer scene on the other. Every time I look at this vase on my bookshelf in the living room, I think of him. Late at night when I'm all alone I could swear that it moves a little. And so I say, "Hello, Ted, how are you doing? I send my Love and Light to you."

Chapter 7

GHOST OF THE MARK CLARK EXPRESSWAY

In 1989 a private detective, Howie Comen, came to me at the request of one of his clients, the wife of a missing highway inspector, Ralph Terry Griggs. Howie was truly a non-believer and Lori Griggs, the missing inspector's wife, really had to prod him to come to our office. He had always believed that psychics were just somebody to make jokes about. I didn't take too kindly to the joking way he greeted me and my office staff. After all, most people weren't quite as outspoken as this Connecticut Yankee.

However, it wasn't long till Howie had made friends with my whole family and went on to be one of the best friends I would ever have in this life. He had met with me several times and I had tranced and allowed my guardian angel, Catherine of Siena, to come through and give us messages about Terry Griggs' death. Catherine had already told us that Terry would not be found. However, she had given us a lot of information about discrepancies on the cross-town expressway, the Mark Clark, named after the great South Carolina Military General. She had even given us a specific page number of a five thousand-page state contract to look at. Howie immediately called the governor's office and a friend of his who was an aide there had it hand-carried to us.

Just as we had predicted, in later years, we would find out that the joints would fail due to shoddy workmanship on the bridge. Fifteen hundred pilings would have to be replaced in one area alone because they had been put into the marsh the wrong way. This would cost the taxpayers another nine million dollars. The state senator, Ernie Passailaigue, listened to us and had the bridgework closed down and the repairs made.

Lori Griggs was grieving terribly and so was her young daughter over the mystery surrounding their missing husband

and father. No one seemed to be helping whatsoever. Everyone was just sort of keeping quiet. In all fairness to the police, there was not much that could be done since they just could not find the body. There is an old saying I've heard among cops, "No body, no case." Some rumors were spread that he just took off and left town, which Lori refused to believe.

One night, shortly after I started working with Howie, I was talking with him on the phone. It was late at night and he had phoned to discuss the case with me.

I remember saying to him, "Howie, I hate this kind of work. There is too much foul play; furthermore, police work does not mix well with the vibrations I am trying to set up in order to work with my clients."

"Oh, kid, you will be okay. Get some rest and we'll talk further in the morning," he said.

After hanging up the phone, I lay down on my stomach and rested my head on my nice, clean rose-printed pillow and closed my eyes intending to sleep. I had just put my notebook and pen in the bottom drawer of my nightstand. All of a sudden, I opened my eyes for a minute looking over to a place where I sensed something going on in my bedroom. I felt a presence, something or someone who didn't belong there in my private space. Then I saw this huge man with a head, which appeared to be shaven; the hair had begun to grow out again so there were only dark stubs that I could see. He was something to look at — a gruesome person who I would have been afraid of if I had met him on the street. However, at this moment I was more startled than afraid. I had never had a victim of a murder appear to me. Or had I? Then I remembered the spirit of John in California and felt that his visit was just a sample of the work I would be doing in the future, exorcisms and solving murders of dead people who would appear to me. There was nothing compared to getting the straight scoop from the victim himself.

He spoke: "Please write what I tell you!"

I looked and to my surprise, there were no lights on but there was an enormous light from his body. My notebook and pen were there on my bed. I was shocked since I had just put them carefully in the drawer. He gave me five pages of information. He alluded to the man who had him murdered and how he was killed. He tried to tell me where his body was but I could not understand all of the information. Much of the information was in symbols except for the name of the person who had him killed and the business owners who were involved. He actually told me the name of the businesses. He specifically named two businesses.

I stopped writing and phoned Howie. "Howie, he's here! Terry Griggs is here!" I screamed.

"That's great, let's call Lori and tell her he's alright!" He didn't know what I meant.

"No, I mean his ghost is here and he's telling me to write all this information down. Howie, I don't want to know all this!"

"Then let's get the hell off the phone so you can listen to him! What are you doing on the phone with me when he is there giving you the whole lowdown on his death? Hang up the damn phone and listen to him!"

So I continued to write down everything he told me. The next morning I took all the information to the FBI and to the Charleston County Police. They knew the men Terry was talking about but they said they could do nothing unless we could find the body. Without the body there was no evidence. They knew these businessmen were corrupt but could not indict them for a murder when they did not have a body.

Howie and I went to the different construction companies to see if they would check the pilings where Terry's body might be but they did not want anything to do with us. They were actually afraid of us. They had good reason because they were being extremely ridiculed about their alleged shoddy workmanship, which the ghost of Terry Griggs had alluded to.

We took our information to every police department but no one would help at all or even give us any advice. The only police who were remotely interested was the Charleston County Police who could do nothing. It was out of their jurisdiction.

The missing car had been found in Berkeley County. The policeman, whom this case had been assigned to, would not even have a meeting with me for fear of being laughed at, I suppose.

Terry visited me often after this and one time he appeared outside my window in my home, which overlooked a marsh. The Mark Clark Expressway was visible too. He said, "Eenie, meenie, minee, moe, catch a n----- by his toe."

I took it to mean that the man who was responsible for shutting out his last breath was African American. He then showed me a big African-American man who he had worked with. Lori, his wife, had told me that he was very prejudiced toward minorities even though he worked and associated with them everyday. The man who he showed us earlier who had put out the "contract" on Terry's life was a white man. This murder has never been solved.

Terry continued to come to me with added information. His last visit was eight months ago. He came through while I was reading for one of Howie's clients. He told us that he was killed by the big sharks and finished off by the little fish. I knew this was not only symbolic but was also literal because it fit some of the other information he had given me the first time his ghost appeared in my bedroom.

He told us a woman's name and told us to get in touch with her. He informed us she knew all the details of his murder. We turned this information over to the police in charge of the case. I even told them where the woman lived. They knew about her and said they would go visit and question her but never did. As a matter of fact, the policemen in charge of the case now have done nothing to solve the case... in all honesty, they are overwhelmed with unsolved cases and they put this one at the end of their list of priorities, especially since no one ever came up with the body and probably no one ever will. Terry's spirit says he was hung up like a hog in a freezer. There is much more information if any of the police or authorities ever have guts enough to use this information to force the culprits to come forward and confess. It would surely help a young woman who has just given birth to her father's (the missing Ralph Terry Griggs) first grandchild who is the "spitting" image of him.

I haven't heard from Terry in quite some time, so maybe he has reincarnated to be with his family again, especially his young daughter who he loved as much as he was capable of loving.

Last year, my name appeared on the front page of the local newspaper, saying, "I TOLD YOU SO!" The joints have been coming up all over the bridges and many truckers and other drivers have complained to the highway department. A number of vehicles, I understand, have been damaged from the joints Terry had warned us about on the Mark Clark Expressway.

I believe Terry will continue to come to me in the future until something has been done about his death. He always says, "Check the joints." I also believe the discrepancies on the expressway will continue to appear until the murderers of this man have been punished. I call Terry the "ghost of the Mark Clark Expressway."

However, I hope through all the prayers that his friends and family have said for him that he is either in the Light with God or that he has returned to his family through this wonderful little baby boy. God Bless You, Terry... wherever you are!

Chapter 8

GHOST OF GRANDMOTHER ASKS FORGIVENESS FOR LYNCHING

I have experienced the fact that after a hurricane or tornado, there seems to be a purifying effect of the catastrophe on communities and people's lives. Maybe God uses these types of things to clean out the gutters of our minds, our homes, and our communities. Also, I believe He uses it to show us His power and strength in order to help us all be more humble before Him. Who knows? Many in Charleston, South Carolina seem to believe this was what happened after Hurricane Hugo.

It was shortly after this hurricane had hit our town in September of 1989, that I received a call from a local therapist. She asked me to come to her home to verify that it was haunted and to offer help. An apparition had been seen at the top of her stairs many times... not only by Janie, the owner of the home, but by some of her friends who visited this home quite often. She could not figure out if it was a woman or a man but she knew it needed to be dealt with.

Her house was one of those big old white wooden homes with the big pillars, which you see on television quite often depicting the essence of the South. In the 1800s, this was the typical plantation home. By the time I got to the appointment I had there, the home had been almost completely rebuilt from the damage it suffered by the ravages of the hurricane.

When we reached her home, I saw a television news van parked in front. When we rang the doorbell, Michael answered the door; the same cameraman who had filmed an exorcism I had done with Ted Knight, star of *Action Line*, a show to help victims of fraud or to help people with problems they could not seem to solve themselves.

"Michael, what are you doing here?"

I was surprised when I saw his face. He had been the only cameraman who had ever filmed one of my exorcisms. What a coincidence!

"Well, I just started dating Janie," he answered. I told her to call you since she was so troubled about this ghost who has been appearing ever since her divorce," he explained.

Howie and I went into the living room and sat down. I prayed for guidance. I then asked Janie for a picture of her grandmother.

"How do you know it's my grandmother haunting me?" she asked curiously.

"I'm a professional medium. Isn't that why you called me here? For the expertise I have attained in my field?" I replied laughingly.

I held the picture in my hand and told her that her grandmother was a troubled woman before she died and she needed to be released into the Light. "She is asking me to get her rocking chair from the parlor and take it up to the room which has been empty for so long."

"Oh, my God! This is unbelievable! We have a room that was empty and I just made it into my son's room. Michael, get her rocking chair. It's right in the next room there by the door," she said, quite stunned at what she'd heard.

I asked if I could consult the spirit of Catherine first before we left to go upstairs. Communicating through a deep trance, Catherine gave us more information, which made everything clearer to me and reassured me that I was on the right path.

Because Janie, the owner of the home, was Catholic, she ran over to touch Catherine through me. Howie had to pull me out of the trance. It is very dangerous if someone tries to touch the medium while in trance. Edgar Cayce, a famous trance medium of the early part of the century once said, "Don't touch me when I'm in a trance because I will surely have to come out of trance and protect my body."

"Hail Mary, full of Grace, pray for us sinners now and at the time of our death," she was reciting the rosary.

She cried and cried for Catherine to help her. It frightened me! I couldn't accept her adoration even if it was for a spirit coming through me. I am very careful to not allow people to make me their Messiah. I am not worthy of that kind of treatment and I must always remember that only God is worthy of worshipping and that includes Catherine. Catherine herself reminds us all the time that she is not to be worshipped. She refers to herself as a lowly nun, trying to do her part to make the Universe a better place to be.

Howie, Michael, Janie and I proceeded upstairs. As soon as I stepped into the room, I sat down in the chair and started rocking as if I were being pulled into a trance by this old grandmother. Catherine had warned us not to allow her to take over my body; however, it all happened too fast. She was already there. It was strange! It was as if I were a Siamese twin to this old woman. She would speak and I would listen.

"1936! 1936! I ran over an old black woman with my car!" she shouted. "I'm afraid of going to hell so I stay around here," she said.

"You are already dead!" Howie reminded her.

"How could you, Mammy? My family knew you deliberately ran over that old woman; they have talked about it for years. Shame on you! No wonder you are afraid of letting go!" her granddaughter said with tears streaming down her face.

"That's not all, I had that black man lynched when I told the authorities he raped me! He didn't rape me! My daddy did, over and over again all during my childhood! I had to get back at my daddy and this is the only way I could find to do it!"

"Mammy, how could you do all these things!" Janie shouted.

"One more confession: Your grandfather is not your father's daddy. I had an affair with your Uncle Ben. That's his father," she told Janie. "Oh, God, I've sinned and I've sinned!" her spirit cried.

"Jesus is waiting for you!" called Howie, my Jewish friend who was empathetically trying to bring her peace of mind through her Christian religion she was still holding onto. It was a sight to behold.

Then all of a sudden, this thirty-nine-year-old woman who was a real professional cried out to her dead grandmother with pain.

"Oh, Mammy, Mammy, please bond with me. You never hugged me. You never kissed me. I wanted so much for you to love me." Janie cried like the little girl she had been when her grandmother was alive.

"Go into the Light, go into the Light!" shouted Howie. But she could not go into the Light until Janie released her by releasing her bitterness and hatred for her grandmother. Her negativity was holding her to this earth plane.

Janie promised to seek out hypnotherapy for herself so that all this could be resolved in her mind. This was my advice to her. Her grandmother's presence was evident no more. I got up from the rocking chair and started walking toward the stairs.

"Hey, wait a minute, there's another ghost visitor here and this is one that you will have to let go. It's a young man a little older than yourself. He's clean-cut and looks like he has been a Citadel cadet. He says for you to get some swings like the both of you had as a child and remember him when you are swinging!" I told her.

"Oh, that's my brother. I always imagined him to look like one of the Citadel cadets. Just yesterday Michael and I looked at swings for the backyard but they had to be just the kind I had when I was a child. Oh, I can't let him go. I want him to be with me," she cried out.

"You must let him go. These are the ghosts of your childhood. Take the beautiful memories with you but, my dear, please let these lost souls go into the Light so that they can have their own future! You must! You must! It is selfish to hold on to these souls; they do not belong to you! They belong to God."

"I promise, I'll do my best! You don't know what this has meant to me, Ms. Baron, thank you and Howie so much. I'll never forget tonight!" she said as we left.

Howie and I were dumbfounded as we drove home. "I can't believe that I am so honored to see these things, Elizabeth," he told me. Every time I think I am beginning to understand what you do, I get the shock of my life with something else that is a thousand times more amazing than the last. Thanks for letting me be a part of it," he said in an almost sacred and humbled voice.

As I got out of his car at my door, I looked back at him and smiled, "Ah, Howie, it's all in a day's work!"

"Well, kid, it looks like you and I could become real, honest-to-goodness ghostbusters before this is all over," and he drove back to the everyday world of his own reality, his wife and his two young sons anxiously awaiting his return.

Chapter 9

TRANSMIGRATION OF SOULS

I have learned so much from my guardian angel, St. Catherine of Siena. I had never heard the term" Transmigration of Souls" until Howie and I went to a small southern home to assist four spirits to go into the Light.

According to Webster's Dictionary, the definition of <u>transmigration</u> is as follows: *the passing of individual souls at death into new bodies or different forms of life.*

One day a lady from the suburban town of Mt. Pleasant, South Carolina came to me and asked me if I could come and assist in getting the ghosts out of her home. She told me she had gone out to a movie with her male friend and he had worn her dead husband's hat. Her husband, who was quite a number of years older than she, had died only a few months before, during Hugo Hurricane, which ripped our area apart. He had died of a heart attack.

When they came back, her boyfriend put it back on the hat rack. They both went into another room and when they passed by the hat rack in the dining room, the hat had been moved to the head of the dining room table. She felt her dead husband was haunting the place and that somehow he was angry at her. She also felt he was angrily saying, "I am the head of this house," which was to be disputed later when his spirit was contacted. On the contrary, he would not be an angry spirit at all.

I asked Howie to go with me. Howie was so in awe about all the things I was asked to do with my gift. And we were spending so much time together trying to solve the case of the missing bridge inspector. We were always following any lead we could on that case. We tried to understand some of the symbolic meanings Spirit had given me.

We drove to what looked like a small forty or fifty year old home. There were beautiful old live oaks everywhere, which is typical of the Charleston area. They were so lovely to look at. We who live in this area are privileged to experience the beauty of these old trees each time we drive down a street. The huge trees, lined up on each side of the street, laden with leaves all year round, bend over and meet each other in the middle of the street.

As soon as I entered the house, I felt no warmth, which is typical in a haunted house, only sadness and the presence of unfinished business lingering in the air. There was antique furniture everywhere; in fact there was so much furniture in the living room that we could hardly get to the other rooms. There was a sense of death and a sense of clutter. I felt a great need to organize, to get rid of the furniture. I found later that the furniture, had belonged to the owner's deceased in-laws. I had an urge to replace it with new furniture that was of the present owner's very own choosing. There was a strong sense that she was living almost totally in the past; she was living her in-laws' life. She had not been her true self since moving into this house thirty years ago at the time of her marriage to her husband, a widower. There was real unhappiness there; he had not let go of his dead wife. She would later learn that he never let go. She had lived those many years in this house with her mother-in-law, father-in-law, retarded brother-in-law, her husband and her two sons. Now she was living there with the ghosts of her past.

As soon as Howie and I entered the home, I asked her to take me to the living room. I immediately sat down in a chair, which faced the television.

"That was his chair. He always sat there and watched television," his widow spoke.

I prayed and asked that I would be put in touch with whatever ghosts were haunting the house and that He help me send them all into His Light. As soon as I sat down in the chair, the father of the two sons and the woman's deceased husband began to talk through me. It was if he were just waiting anxiously to be in touch. It was the most beautiful thing I have seen in a long time. He talked with each son and told them that he was proud of them and that he loved them. He said there was so much difference in his age and theirs that he could not always understand their choice of careers and their ways but he asked for forgiveness for that. (One was an artist and the other was sort of an actor). In the dead father's day and time, he had been taught that a man had to have a masculine job, such as carpenter, builder or football player. The sons were so healed from remarks they had never heard from their father when he was living. You could see the looks on their faces that they had made peace with their father.

Then he spoke to his wife. "I'm sorry you had such a rough life with me. You don't have to feel guilty about another man in your life. I never treated you like a wife. You were young and beautiful and I should have treated you better. However, my dead wife kept haunting me. I just could never get over that loss. She is now here with me waiting for me to go with her into the Light. I am leaving you now, but please forgive me, my sons and my wife, and do have a good life!"

That was it! He was gone just like that. He said what he had to say to complete any unfinished business and then he left. The family was more at peace now.

It was not long after that I received another call from Geraldine, the woman who owned the home. This was the same woman who had used my body, mind, and spirit to say goodbye to her dead husband. Her husband had also made peace with his sons who had suffered psychologically from the distance they had felt with their father.

Geraldine informed me that there was another ghost in the house. The living room, which was filled with all those old antiques, had a big bookcase in the corner of the room. It had been locked since 1976. The key had been lost. All of a sudden, it had become unlocked by itself and the doors were swinging open. Of course, this was a symbolic sign to a medium such as myself, just as the hat which had been found at the head of the dining room table was a sign that the husband was trying to tell his family something. These symbolic signs are very pertinent to discovering the reason for a visit from a ghost or spirit.

I rushed back to the house! I seem to be very drawn to exorcisms. It is probably my favorite thing to do with my psychic ability. As soon as I came into the living room, I asked her if I could go back to the bedroom on the far left.

"Yes," she said, as she was just as anxious as I was to get these ghosts on their way.

As suddenly as I entered the bedroom, I became possessed by the dead mother-in-law. This is not a bad possession. I always pray and ask to be surrounded with His White Light before I ever do anything. Then I take the Bible and read the Word. I give the spirit permission to use my body, my mind, and my spirit to get their communication out to their loved ones. I am assured by my guardian angel that I am protected by the Light. I believe in the Higher sources one hundred percent.

The spirit spoke her name. Immediately Geraldine began to cry. "Ashley, I never did anything to you in my life; why did you hate me so?" she begged.

The dead mother-in-law put her hands on her hips and began to answer back. "I'm sorry, I don't know why I treated you badly. I guess I missed Frank's first wife and knew that he did too, so I just never could accept another wife. It didn't have anything to do with you and I am sorry," she explained.

They talked a while longer and then I asked her to go onto God with her son and his first wife. She did. Geraldine looked as though a ton of bricks had been lifted off her back. It was so wonderful to see the peace that she displayed and I thanked God that I could be a part of such a wonderful experience.

To help the deceased and the living to communicate so that the souls can go onto that place we call Heaven; to allow the living to bury the dead and to heal their own wounds are two of the greatest privileges I have ever encountered on my quest to serve God. Heaven is a place where we all will eventually go to rest and not have to worry about what is going on down here on earth. It is where those spirits who have forgiven and been forgiven are truly at peace and do not communicate any longer with us. That is, unless they are highly evolved and come back to us as our guardian angel, such as Catherine came to me.

Unfortunately, this was just the beginning of some more serious problems in this house that we (Howie and I) just did not know how to handle by ourselves. We would soon learn this and have to consult with my guardian angel, Catherine of Siena, who was older and wiser and could explain the unknown to us.

There was subsequently another visit to Geraldine's home. This time we would find yet another ghost, the spirit of her retarded brother-in-law. She led me to his room and I allowed his spirit to slip into my body. "I want a Coca-Cola; I want my Daddy!" he began to shout.

I lay down on the floor and sort of wallowed on the small rug, which lay in front of the bed. "Your Daddy isn't here, Gene," Geraldine spoke.

"Elizabeth, he was always asking for a Coke. I guess he was addicted to them. He would never come out of his room unless his Daddy gave him permission. You see, he was fifty three; however, he had the mind of a five year old boy," she explained.

I asked Howie to call my name — to call me back to my real self and to allow me to have Gene let go of my body.

"I don't know, Geraldine, I don't know how to get this person into the Light. I guess he only does what his Daddy tells him to do. However, if I trance and let my guardian angel, St. Catherine come through, she can tell us. I don't know where his Daddy is. He's not in this house like the rest of his family's ghosts. So I have to find him first," I explained to her. We promised to come again.

In the meantime, I tranced and allowed Catherine to come through and give us information on the whereabouts of the father-in-law.

She explained it this way: "When a soul dies and does it unwillingly, sometimes, if there is a weak body or a young body in the house, instead of dying, the soul just goes over to the baby's body and lives with that baby's soul. This is called

Transmigration of Souls. Ask your Rabbi about it, Howie. He will explain."

Howie went to the Rabbi and he referred him to a part of the Bible where this had happened to one of God's prophets.

Later, we shared this with Geraldine: The father-in-law is in the body of the six-month-old baby who was in the house at the time of his death.

"Yes, my oldest son was six months old when his grandfather died," she answered.

"But Catherine, we can't get this young man to come here," Howie told her.

"Never mind, let me take care of that! He will be here when he needs to be here," Catherine's spirit promised us.

A reporter for one of the local newspapers had come along with us and had written an article about this phenomenon. Soon a New York news reporting television show picked it up in a newspaper clipping service. They contacted my office and wanted to come down to film a real exorcism. I explained to them what was happening, that I had already exorcised the mother-in-law and the father. There were two more ghosts, the brother-in-law and the father-in-law. However, I could not find the spirit of the father-in-law. They wanted to come anyway. So we made arrangements for them to come that next week.

The next week we all gathered in the little home where I, along with the family, had witnessed two spirits going into the Light. Now, the television producers would try and film what they could of the other two spirits going into the Light; that is if I could find the father-in-law's spirit.

I sat down and explained to them and to Geraldine that the only way I could get the father of the retarded brother-in-law to help him to go into the Light was to have the oldest son, Mac, there. He didn't really believe in what I was doing, even though he had derived peace from talking to his dead father. I told the producer we would wait a few minutes and try and figure out what to do.

The producer and others went outside the house for a smoke. While they were gone, I decided to go sit in the living room where the cameras were all set up to film any part of the exorcism they could get on film. There sat Mac, the oldest son.

I was so shocked even though St. Catherine had said that she would make sure he was there. Our little minds kept wondering... how could the spirit of a fourteenth century nun get a guy to do what he didn't want to do. I ran outside to gather the camera crew back into the house. I sat down in Gene's (the retarded brother-in-law's) chair and I asked Mac if he would come over and sit in a chair that had belonged to his grandfather in those bygone days.

"Mac, did you know your retarded Uncle Gene?" I asked him.

"Of course I did, he lived with us for many years after my grandparents died," he said.

"Would you like to see your Uncle go into the Light of God?" I asked him.

"I sure would. This is so disturbing to my mother," he mentioned.

"Okay, I'm going into trance and I will allow your Uncle Gene to take over my body. As soon as he speaks, would you just say over and over to him, 'Uncle Gene, go into the Light; Uncle Gene, go into the Light!' Don't stop saying that until you feel at peace."

I began to go into a deep trance by first asking my Creator to protect my body, mind and spirit and then to allow Uncle Gene to use those bodies to communicate. Mac began to shout, "Uncle Gene, please go into the Light!" All of a sudden, there was a strong vibration, almost like a strong wind in my body, moving out and beyond me. At the same time, the spirit of the grandfather that was possessing Mac's body rushed to meet his retarded son and they both went together to meet their Creator! It was beautiful, and even though the people there could not see these entities, they could feel the peaceful feeling that inundated the home of Geraldine. No longer would she have to live with her dead family. The house belonged to her and her two sons and they were truly at peace!

That was in 1989. I see them all often in Charleston when I pass their places of business and we share warm thoughts of those days of the cleansing of spirits in their home!

Chapter 10

MOTORCYCLE ACCIDENT BRINGS COUPLE TOGETHER FOREVER

One evening, back in 1990, a middle-aged, attractive woman came to one of my St. Catherine trance sessions. On Sunday evening for many years, I would invite my clients into my office and I would allow the spirit of my guardian angel, St. Catherine, to come through and give them messages. Many people who had lost loved ones would come in hopes their deceased family would come through and let them know they were alright; that they had made it over to the other side... it would help them so much to finish up their grieving process. Sometimes, there would be as many as over one hundred people and they would all get individual messages from Catherine; messages that were pertinent to what was going on in their lives.

I remember one time I was at a hotel banquet room and I lay down and allowed Catherine to come through and give all these people messages. The huge room held all 140 people who were waiting for a message. One of these messages happened to be for a Senator's wife who I had never met.

"Please do not divorce your husband," Catherine asked her. "He won't be living very long, so let him enjoy his family while he is still here."

I received a phone call from a reporter of the local paper in that town later. She told me the Senator's wife was so shocked. She told the reporter no one knew that she was thinking of divorcing her husband except herself. She had not mentioned it to a soul.

On this Sunday night at my home, another middle-aged, attractive lady looked at me with mystery and awe in her eyes when she came through my door and I greeted her. She also looked at me with skepticism. While I was allowing St. Catherine to take over my body, Catherine told her that her eighteen-year-old son was over on the other side and that he had a message for her. He had been killed on the expressway and he had a young lady, whom he barely knew, on the back of his motorcycle. As a matter of fact, they had just met each other that night. They had hit a steel railing and both instantly died.

Her son told her he was sorry to cause her grief; however, he said that he and the girl had a strong karmic tie to past lives they had shared together. They were happy to be together on the "other side." There they were, perhaps together for eternity.

The mother was pleased with the message but it had been too much for her. She continued to grieve for a long time. She just really could not get over her only son leaving at such a young age. She came to me for several readings and continued visiting his grave and probably still does. I tried to get her to come to my meditation classes which would have helped her to get her own messages; they would have helped her also to eventually let her son go. We cannot hold onto the dead. It certainly doesn't help the dead and it won't help us either. Certain tribes of the American Indians believe that it is good and healthy to grieve for a year; however, after that, they believe one is just feeling sorry for self.

I have been giving these meditation classes for more than twenty years now. It really helps others not only to let go of the past, but also to understand that there is a life beyond this one. I am now also teaching channeling classes and even my eleven-year-old granddaughter can do channeling. Yes, channeling can be learned when the student is ready. You know, like the old saying, "When the student is ready, the teacher appears." Just remember, the seeker's motives are important and one must surround oneself with the Holy Light.

I stopped doing the trances with my guardian angel, Catherine each month because it seemed that the same people were coming, getting messages and advice but not doing much with the messages. I felt I was not helping these people at all. I now realize that this was not for me to judge and will begin again soon to channel more. Now I do life readings and we go to the spirit of St. Catherine to get advice for the police or when we really feel that we need some serious guidance on a matter. I also go to her for the very important prophecies she gives around the end of December for each New Year. About seventy-five percent of these prophecies have been accurate since 1987. Sometimes it is frightening to do these prophecies, knowing there is a seventy-five per cent chance that they will come true.

Chapter 11

SUICIDE VICTIM REGRETS HANGING HIMSELF

On a hot summer day in the low country of South Carolina around 1991, a young eighteen-year-old boy was so troubled after he had returned home from prison. He had been serving time for raping a young woman who had later confessed to friends that he indeed did not rape her. She was his girlfriend and was very angry that he had broken off his friendship with her. We all have to be careful what we say about others, lest we do so much harm which could stay with the victim for the rest of their life.

This young man's name was Billy. After being released from prison he could not find a job. No one would hire him when they found out he had a prison record. As if that problem was not great enough for him, there was another one that was just as serious. He began dating the daughter of a policeman. It was alleged that the policeman and his wife had vowed he would never get another job. They would speak to the prospective employer and blackball him if they found he was applying for a job at a certain place. They told the employer he had a police record. The family told me he was continually arrested and had spent much time in a hospital trying to heal from the wounds of alleged police abuse. This was information given to me by the mother and sister of the young man. I cannot verify it.

One night he decided to call the police. It seemed that he felt there was no way out of his dilemma. "By the time you get to my house, I will be dead," he had said on the recording, according to his family. When they arrived only minutes later, there he was... hanging in a tree in the backyard with his dog looking on, howling like a wolf at the young man's body.

They took him to a small town in North Carolina and buried him, only to find in a few weeks that his spirit did not stay with the body. His spirit had returned home with the family. Billy was sorry he had taken his own life, he was telling his sister.

As phenomena began to build up in the house, the mother and the sister invited me over to visit them. They lived on John's Island, an old area of Charleston where the practice and belief of voodoo and black magic is still alive and well; something which was a carryover from the native African tribes who had been brought to the South as slaves ages ago. This is something that is not only practiced by local African Americans but also the white race as well. As I drove down this beautiful live oak lined road, I could feel the vibrations of the slaves working in the rice plantations in this area. Today this area consists of farming tomatoes, strawberries, and other crops, which are harvested mostly by the Mexican young people who are brought in for that purpose. There are little houses lined up in certain areas of the island where they live while they bring in the crops. Of course, this island has made many changes as property in our area becomes more scarce. Many people have moved onto John's Island and built beautiful homes; therefore property is now extremely valuable. Nonetheless, the vibrations of long ago still haunt the area.

Billy had lived in a small room in his parents' home. The furniture in his room consisted of a double bed, a chest of drawers and a small chest with a stereo on top of it. Each night, according to the mother, the stereo would begin to play the song, "Tears From Heaven" by Eric Clapton. It played, unassisted by anyone. The mother would take the tape out of the stereo, only to find it had been put back in by unseen hands the next day, playing away this favorite song of the deceased.

The family asked if I would help in any way. I knew this was something I needed to do. Of course, in my position, there was no one to do this for them but me. First, I found they had no money for the burial. They were very poor and had no insurance on the young man's life. I arranged along with the help of a very nice news director at a local television station to sell some of my prints (I am also a professional artist) to help defray the expenses of the funeral. This helped with other donations, which came in via the news on television.

Finally, after a few days, the spirit of this young man was so strong (it seemed that his strength was building up stronger and stronger) that the mother and sister would see him lying on the living room sofa watching television, just as he had done before he died.

None of the above would have been so awful had he not also chosen to continue as he had before death to tease his brother-in-law terribly. Ray, a Vietnam veteran, suffered terribly from post-traumatic stress disorder. His wife, the sister of the deceased was pregnant. He would come to Ray often and tell him that he was going to reincarnate into his child soon. They were not friendly at all before his death and Ray certainly did not want to see Billy come back into this life as his very own son. The thought of it really frightened this young veteran.

Finally, we decided to do an exorcism. Everyone wanted to be there. There were television cameras everywhere. People from all over had brought food and so the dining room table was full of goodies to eat. Southern people are extremely kind when one of their neighbors is in trouble. Signs of this southern hospitality was certainly evident here.

Billy's younger brother was there. Just as I was getting ready to go into the bedroom and do the exorcism, Jim came up to me.

"Ms. Baron, you will be back over here in a month because one month from today, I am going to be with my brother," he exclaimed.

"Jim, how could you do that to your mother? Can't you see how she is suffering from the loss of your brother? How could you even think such a thing?" I asked him.

"Mark my word, I'll be dead one month from today!" he kept saying. We all should have taken him seriously and he should have been taken to a psychiatrist. However, the family was so upset over the present suicide, they hardly could think of the possibility of another one.

I walked into Billy's bedroom and lay down to prepare for the exorcism. I prayed for protection from anything negative that might obstruct my work. As usual, I had fasted for a few days to cleanse not only my body but my mind. I thanked God for my gift and then I proceeded to go ahead with the exorcism.

I allowed Billy's spirit to come through and say goodbye to his loved ones; one by one, he spoke with each family member, telling them he loved them and that he missed them. Each of them cried; you could see the sadness on their faces and feel the pain in their quivering voices as they let go of their loved one, their brother and son. Then I saw a spirit who had joined him. When I described the spirit to the family, they informed me that it was his grandfather. The spirit of the grandfather took his hand and led him over to the other side. We all cried a little and then said a prayer of thanks that he was safe at home on the "other side."

Exactly one month from that day, I got a call from the mother. "Ms. Baron, remember what Jim told you about going to meet his brother? Well, this morning we discovered that he also had hanged himself on his front porch just like Billy was found in my oak tree in the backyard. He's gone! But I think he's better off. He is with his brother who he missed terribly and for some reason I feel at peace, even though the pain is tremendous!"

Jim never haunted the family like Billy did. We felt confident that Billy and his grandfather's spirits had been there to help him cross over!

Chapter 12

GHOST OF JACO INTRODUCES US TO FRIENDS IN NEW YORK CITY

In 1990, my daughter Sandy had met a nice young Italian man who had just completed his tour of duty with the U.S. Navy and was living in Summerville, South Carolina, a suburb of Charleston. Flavio began coming to our meditation group, which we held on Sunday evening. One night, I asked him if he would like to go to my daughter's house where she was having a Labor Day party. He was thrilled since he had spent most of his time out to sea and didn't know too many people.

He had recently been divorced. I was extremely impressed when I heard him pray at the meditation group, "Please dear God, help me to be both mother and father to my children until I find the mother who you have chosen for them."

I surprised Sandy by bringing him with me and I introduced him to her and my other two daughters, Theresa and Gretchen. He immediately gravitated toward Sandy.

He was a bass guitarist and he was delighted when he found that Sandy was also a guitarist and a singer/songwriter. Soon, they were meeting almost every night, not just to get acquainted but to also "jam" with other musicians. It wasn't long before he and Sandy got together and they began sharing expenses, their love and the responsibility of his two lovely children, of whom he had custody. It would not be long until they began planning their wedding. And so they went right to work, making the extra upstairs room into a musician's studio.

One night Sandy called me. "Mom, you need to get right over here; there's a ghost in this house." I could not come right away but on Saturday night, a few days later I did go, along with some of my friends. If there are friends around you when you are communicating with ghosts, it helps a lot... that is if they believe in the paranormal. You can use their energy as well as yours to bring that spirit through and find its purpose for making a visit into that home.

As I sat down on the floor in the studio along with my friends, this amazing personality, Jaco Pastorius, a famous bass player, who once played with groups, such as Blood, Sweat and Tears and Weather Report, came through. Sometimes he was cursing and sometimes he would take on an altogether different personality.

"I need to forgive my mom and dad," he said. He went on to say that they had pulled the plug on him before he had the chance to come back and play my music. He was only in a coma about nine days and then they pulled the plug. "Man, that was awful! Now I'm stuck over here. I want to play my music," he would say. "Someone stole my damn music; someone stole it, could you believe it? I want it published and I want my twin sons to be able to have some money, along with my daughter and my older son. There's a guy who will call you for a reading in a few days, Elizabeth; his name is Ken. He will guide you to my friends and my family. Let me tell you something... they may knock my teeth down my throat and leave me for dead but they can't stop me. I'm here to prove it!" he continued.

Within three days, the man named Ken called. He was the manager of a band in England but he was from New York.

"Ken, do you know someone by the name of Jaco?" I asked him. "His spirit is coming through and he told us you would be able to introduce us to his friends."

"Sure I know Jaco Pastorius, the famous musician. He was one of the best bassists in his business, perhaps **the** best. I was going to be his new manager before he got killed. By the way, do you have the tape recorder on? You are making history right now, you know!" he shouted.

"No, but I can turn the tape recorder on now," I told him.

"Call my ex-wife; she works at Elektra Records. She knows some of Jaco's friends. Tell her to put you in touch with Rita. He was very close to her. By the way, how did he get down to your daughter's boyfriend's house?" he asked curiously.

"Well, it's a long story. Flavio is from Brooklyn, New York. He used to go watch Jaco perform at the Blue Note. He and my daughter went to New York to meet his parents because Flavio and Sandy are getting married. Flavio made a bass guitar, which was exactly like Jaco's; so you might say Flavio was somewhat obsessed with being a musician like Jaco. We believe this is why Jaco appeared to him," I replied.

"I know that Valerie, my ex-wife, Rita and Jaco's other friends have tried to contact his spirit for many years through mediums in New York, but to no avail," Ken informed me.

As soon as I finished my conversation with Ken, I was on the phone with Valerie, Ken's ex-wife. Valerie immediately put me in touch with Rita Guzman, who had been one of Jaco's best platonic friends.

Soon after, Rita flew to Charleston. We immediately went to Flavio and Sandy's music studio. When Jaco came through this time, he acted like an entirely different person. He spoke through me as if something was wrong with him... it appeared that he may have had psychological problems. Rita immediately explained that he'd suffered from manic depression. His behavior was bizarre and he would do strange things like curling up under a table and hanging out at the basketball courts, not having slept in days, urinating on the sidewalks of New York. In spirit, nothing had changed; he continued to do strange things like that. He asked Rita to help him keep the thieves from profiting from his music.

She explained that just before he died, he was playing in a nightclub and a man came in and recorded his music on a small tape recorder. After he had died, the man took the tape to Japan. At that time, it was one of the top albums in Japan. However, his family had not received one dime from the royalties.

This communication with Jaco was in 1990. Since that time, Jaco has grown spiritually. He was a Catholic before he died. He has spoken some very spiritual words to us since then. He has led us to his son, John and we have brought messages to him from his father; to his friend Geri Palladino; his friend Marilyn;

Victor, a drummer; and many, many others whom he played with when he was here.

Sandy and Flavio eventually moved to New York City and many of these people who knew Jaco became their friends as well as mine. He has given us many messages from his friends on the other side, including Ricky Nelson, Miles Davis and others.

We appreciate him so. He still comes now and then but his messages are not as strong. Perhaps he has found the Light.

Through this contact with Jaco, I met his close friend Geri Palladino, who led me to not only the Palace Theatre ghosts but to the New York City Ballet kids, (as I call them), to the St. James Theatre and to a host of new friends we have made over the years. Jaco was used by Spirit to help heal all these people's wounds and to let us all know that life-after-life is a reality.

Chapter 13

THE GHOST OF ABRAHAM LINCOLN SPEAKS TO ME

One night I was teaching a dialoguing class. This class consists of each student writing a letter to someone they would like to communicate with. It could be God, a spirit of a loved one, or it could be a living being. It doesn't matter; the main thing is that the student has something to learn from that person or maybe something to settle with them. St. Catherine taught me how to do this. During the fourteenth century, she wrote a book called, *The Dialogue*, which consisted of conversations with God and it is still being published today. She told me to teach my students how to do this and I have been doing it for over twenty years now.

Many new writers of today's society have copied her book by having their own dialogue with God and I'm sure this is what she intended when she wrote it; that we might all have our personal communication with the Creator.

We were all sitting in a circle in my New Life Center, a teaching center, my daughter, Sandy and I had established many years ago which still exists in Charleston, South Carolina. We were all writing away, dialoguing with different people or entities. I had asked if a positive spirit would come through and give me some guidance. All of a sudden, instead of writing on the paper, there was a Presence in front of me. He spoke profoundly.

"Well, little lady, you seemed to have bitten off more than you can chew by yourself, so we all came down to help you," he spoke with that southern Illinois dialogue I was so familiar with. After all, I had lived in Illinois for most of my adult life... "My name is Abe," he continued.

"Is that you? President Abraham Lincoln?" I asked, strangely puzzled that he would visit me in front of all these students. I was so embarrassed. I was whispering so that I would not disturb their writing.

"That's me, alright. I'm here, along with Andy Jackson, St. Francis of Assisi, and old Martin. He's here, even though you don't like him."

"You mean, Martin Luther King? I do indeed like him. I just don't like the fact that he cheated on his wife," I said, terribly embarrassed that he had read my mind, for I had surely never expressed to anyone that I didn't like "Old Martin."

"Mr. President, did John Wilkes Booth murder you? Are you still in the White House?" I asked a number of questions quickly for fear that he would leave before I could spill out to him all the unanswered mysteries which still surround his death.

"Well, John Wilkes Booth may have pulled the trigger, but those old plantation owners are responsible for my death. They just did not want their tradition of owning slaves to stop. Yes, I am still in the White House, I have to try and keep those old codgers in line up there. Remember, we are here with you if you need us."

This message frightened me and I knew that my life was in danger, due to a lot of police cases I was working on. I acted as quickly as I could and protected my family with insurance policies and then I went on working on the cases I had been assigned to by my spirit... murders, exorcisms, missing persons, life readings. The truth is that if you are afraid to stand up for what you believe, there really isn't any need to be here on this earth.

We all have a special purpose for being here and I have been assured by my spirit guides and by Catherine that I will be here till my work is completed.

Chapter 14

THE GHOST OF JOHN F. KENNEDY ASKS A FAVOR

It was a beautiful Sunday morning when this wonderful thing happened to me. Charleston, my home is one of the most beautiful cities in the world. It is filled with culture and history every where you look. I was sitting in my art studio, which overlooked the Charleston Harbor. I could see all the huge yachts and the small cruisers taking off, making their way out into the ocean to enjoy the lovely weather we are always so fortunate to have; that is except for the hurricanes. But today was the typical beautiful Sunday morning. It was sunny and warm outside and cool inside my air-conditioned studio. There were beautiful white egrets sitting in the marsh, little brown rabbits running across the back yard with their new babies following after them. What a sight to see!

As I sat there, trying to finish up an oil painting of the Blessed Virgin Mary, all of a sudden, I felt a presence. I was no longer alone. One of my spirit friends had come to visit me.

Suddenly I heard this man's voice speaking to me. He had a certain New England accent that was all too familiar.

"I need you to do me a favor," he exclaimed, as if he had always known me. "I need you to go to my family and tell them..." and then he went on. He began to give me messages that I would never reveal publicly because they were very private things he wanted his family to know. Then he disappeared before I could say anything.

Two weeks later, I was sitting in my art studio; working on the very same painting of the Mother Mary.

"You didn't do what I asked you to do," he said with a somewhat disappointed sound in his voice.

"Mr. President, I couldn't do that. Do you realize that my trying to get in touch with your family would be like my trying to have an audience with the Queen of England. I'm just not important enough to take up their time," I told him.

"You are wrong; I'm going to tell you how to get in touch with them and it's important that you follow through on this. Tomorrow morning, go outside and look in your driveway. Pick up your newspaper and turn to page 2 and there will be our family lawyer's name. Get his number from Directory Assistance and tell him that John told you to ask him to get in touch with his family. Just give the family member the messages. Please, thank you!" ...and he disappeared.

That night I could hardly sleep while anxiously awaiting to see if his family lawyer's name appeared in the paper. At 6:00 in the morning I heard the delivery woman outside and I ran to the driveway. I opened the *Post & Courier* to page 2 and there it was. There was an article about the Kennedy family right there before me, which included the name of their lawyer.

As soon as the offices opened at 9:00 in the morning, I called his lawyer.

"Sir," I said, "John F. Kennedy's spirit was in touch with me yesterday and he told me to ask you to get in touch with his family. I have a message from him for several members," I nervously informed him.

"Well, my lady, John's my boss and if he told you to do that, then I must follow his orders. Wait right there. Give me your number and someone will call you within the hour," he spoke and then we discontinued our conversation.

Within forty-five minutes, the phone rang. It was one of the Smiths. He explained that Mrs. Kennedy Smith was not well or she would have called. I politely gave them the messages and told them I would not reveal the messages publicly.

They were the nicest people one could imagine. The man told me that I would always be in their prayers. I can tell you this was a joyous experience! I could not believe that this wonderful thing had happened to me! I was given the privilege of delivering a message from the ghost of John Kennedy to his family! This was one of our presidents of the United States of America. I was humble and honored to be of service!

Chapter 15

ALIEN VISITATION SURPRISES ME

There is a lot of talk, among people who are interested and believe in UFOs, that spirits and aliens have much in common. There are many of those people who think they are one and the same. I subscribe to a magazine called *MUFON*, which is sort of the official magazine for UFO interests. I have read a number of times where they have connected spirit phenomena with alien phenomena. I don't know the truth about all this but I would like to convey my experience with aliens here and now.

One morning I was sitting in my art studio painting, just as I was when John F. Kennedy visited me. All of a sudden, my eyes were drawn to the corner of the studio. There they were — these little three feet tall men. All three of them looked just alike. I really would never have been able to tell them apart. They appeared to be frightened; they had a look on their face as if they weren't sure how I was going to respond to them.

They were gray in color and I think they may have had more than five fingers but I'm not sure. I couldn't see or remember that well. After all, when this happens to a person, the person is usually in an altered state of consciousness. They all may have had on a uniform of some kind; however, the gray looked like a skin. They had eyes that slanted up the side of their face and I believe they were black. They had sort of a slit for a mouth and two little holes for nostrils. They seemed to be like kids in their physical appearance but I sensed that they were very old in biological age. Their size made me think of children.

They all spoke at the same time and said through mental telepathy, "We really appreciate what you are doing for the planet."

I responded by saying to them, "Why thank you, that is very nice to hear." At that time, I was giving free meditation lessons, and free advice to the police on murders and missing persons. I was also doing free exorcisms. The only thing I charged for at that time was my life readings and still do at this time. That is how I derive an income. Later I began charging for meditation lessons, feeling the students would appreciate them more if they invested something more than time into the classes.

As quickly as the little aliens came, they disappeared, just like a spirit or a ghost would flash and leave. Afterward, I felt a peace come over me that I had not known for sometime.

I am still just as fascinated and curious about alien life on another planet as you and others may be. This experience only showed me the existence of aliens but I still don't know much more than I did before this experience.

A number of years before this incident back in 1986, I had another experience sort of indirectly with aliens. A psychology teacher here on James Island where I make my home (a suburb of Charleston) came to me and asked me to go about one hundred miles southwest of here to see if I could pick up some vibrations from an alleged spaceship landing. A deputy sheriff's wife had seen a cigar-shaped spaceship land twice on her farmland right beside her house. The house was way out in the country, in a sparsely populated area.

She had told the radio station there that the spaceship landed twice, a few months apart. Shortly after the second landing, two men in black came to her house and showed her some kind of identification. They asked if she had seen the spaceship and if she had seen some sort of animal after the second landing. She told them she had seen a little black dog. They asked her if she knew where the dog was. She informed them that her husband had tied the dog up out near the back of their house in case the owner came looking for it. They asked if they could <u>talk</u> to the dog. This was shocking to her; however, she led them around to the back of the house. She watched from the window.

She said that she watched them talk to the dog and the dog would shake its head yes or no or should I say, up and down and sideways as they asked the dog questions. They then left.

A few weeks later, we went to her house but she would not talk with us at all. She told the teacher that she could never talk about this incident again. We asked her if we could go to the landing site and she agreed. The landing site was just to the left of her home which consisted of a large field, which appeared to have been used for farming.

I lay down on a lounge chair we had brought with us, so that I didn't have to lie on the wet ground. These fields in South Carolina are full of snakes, poisonous as well as others. There were burn spots left in a circle where the landing had taken place. I tranced and asked my Creator to bring forth any information we needed to hear.

There were two other men with us, both very well educated — one who owned a truck dealership and one who held a Ph.D. I breathed myself into a deep trance and was in touch with some sort of entity who had something to do with the landing. They told us they were part of the spaceship phenomena.

"Why don't you show yourselves?" was a question put to them by one of the men who was with us.

"We did show ourselves two thousand years ago and you hung us on a tree," they answered.

"Where do you come from?" the other man asked.

"We come from Andromeda," the space creature replied. "We come to help you protect your planet. We want to show you things we have learned and therefore help to protect the Universe."

There was much more that they told us but I can't remember the exact words. However, this was an experience that was so unusual, I wanted to share it.

Chapter 16

MARY SURRATT DECLARES HER INNOCENCE

In the spring of 1992 a friend of mine and I went to Washington, D.C. We were to meet a man who had seen the ghost of Mary Surratt at Fort McNair, an Army Post in Washington, D.C. He wanted me to see if I could contact her spirit and maybe let her know that she had been forgiven and could now go on into the Light.

This man was a Sgt. in the Army and he had seen the ghost of Mary Surratt going down the hallway of the officer's quarters on the Army post. This old building which now housed officers' families, was once the place of incarceration for Mary Surratt. Alongside the quarters was a huge tennis court. This tennis court was the original place where, Mary Surratt and others were hanged for the assassination of Abraham Lincoln.

The Sgt. told us that the window on the third floor would fog up each day and about every six months they would have to replace it. It was not just a liquid fog; it was some sort of material that could not be scrubbed off. The ghost of Mary Surratt was alleged to have been seen many times, looking out this window with a very sad face and tears in her eyes.

The morning after we arrived at our hotel in Washington, the Sgt. picked us up and drove us to the site of the haunting. It was cold and rainy, the rain mixing with the snow to make a dirty sloppy mess outside along the streets. When we arrived at the site, he pointed to the foggy window and I felt a presence staring down at me even though there was no one visible there. I then chose to go over and sit on one of the benches at the tennis court. The minute I sat down, I realized that there was great painful vibrations left here from the hangings, which took place over one hundred years ago.

The Sgt. said to me, "You are now sitting in the exact place these people were hung. That is where the gallows used to be."

I sat there and prayed for the Holy Spirit to take over my body, mind and spirit as the Sgt. and my friend, Glennis, looked on. I was cold and didn't feel well and since I did not seem to make contact with Mary Surratt's spirit, I got up and began to walk toward the others.

"I just can't do it," I told them. "It's just too cold out here and I feel nothing but pain."

"Okay," the Sgt. answered, "We'll come back another time. I'm sorry I could not get you into the quarters. It would probably be easier if you could physically touch the place where she was incarcerated. However, the Post Commander said it might scare the families in there if they knew some sort of exorcism was taking place. Maybe it will change in the future," he continued as we walked toward his car.

Then something amazing happened. All of a sudden, Mary's spirit completely took me over. "I didn't do it! I didn't do it! Louis will tell you I didn't do it!"

The pain was so great that I began calling to my friend, Glennis, "Glennis, please call me back! She is taking over and I cannot handle the pain she is going through!"

"Elizabeth, Elizabeth, please come out of the trance!" Glennis began to call and I was completely out of the self-induced altered state of consciousness, myself again.

"What did you say, Elizabeth? Did I hear you say, 'Louis will tell you I didn't do it?'" asked the Sgt., who seemed to be in a state of shock.

"Yes, that's what her spirit was saying through me," I answered.

"Wow, do you know anything about the history of Mary Surratt?" he asked.

"No, I have never heard of Mary Surratt until now," I answered him.

"That's amazing because I happen to know a lot about the history of this whole assassination. There was a man named

Louis Paine who was hanged here too and the last thing out of his mouth before they put the hood over his face to hang him was, 'Mary Surratt didn't have anything to do with this and you will find that to be true maybe too late!'"

I hope to go back to this spot sometime in the future and bring Mary through so that she can know that she doesn't have to be there any longer, to let her know that she has permission to go into God's Light through forgiveness and love. At last, she will find the peace she so searches for!

Chapter 17

MANY SPIRITS GATHER IN A WALTERBORO HOME

In the fall of 1992, I was called by a young lady to a place just outside Walterboro, South Carolina because her home was being overwhelmed with ghosts. Walterboro is a small town just southwest of Charleston. The whole town is rather scattered across acreage where farmers still make their living on their small plantations. In the 1800s, this town was the summer colony of many rich plantation owners. Therefore, it is now a big tourist area. Huge, stately, antebellum homes are everywhere.

The young woman was in the process of a divorce and she had just moved to this old, old home on the corner of a street in an urban area. The home did not appear to be very stable. It was built maybe eighty or ninety years ago of wooden structure and swayed to the left a little as if it had been slightly damaged by a hurricane or strong wind at one time. However, there were people still living in it. Years ago, this huge home had been divided into apartments. Not much traffic or activity took place in this part of town. It was an old community inhabited mostly by farmers and country people, some of the most sincere people in the world.

She invited my friends and me upstairs as soon as we got there. I had taken along some of my meditation students who were most interested in exorcisms. We entered the small living room and I could hear faint voices immediately. She told us she was hearing people talk at all hours of the night. She knew the voices did not come from outside. They sounded like they were in the same room we were sitting in.

At last, we all sat down in a circle and each person said a prayer, sending out good wishes for this lovely woman and her young daughter who lived with her. I then went into my usual trance and asked that any spirit who was lost or confused come through and tell us their story. One by one these spirits came, telling us how they came to exist in this house.

There was a young couple who had planned to be married in just a short time. They were killed in an automobile accident near this house. Somehow, they saw the light of the spirits living in this house and joined them, not knowing where they were or how they got there. (It appears that many souls who have accidents are confused when they pass over to the other side quite suddenly. Sometimes they stay out in that limbo state of consciousness until somehow, they are saved by a medium or someone else who has the ability to feel their vibrations.)

There was an old man with white hair who had been a doctor in his lifetime. He was a medical doctor while he was living; He was happy there in that old house and seemed quite content, trying to assist all these people around him.

There were many others too, but I cannot remember all of them. We wished all of them well and sent them into the Light of God. They wanted so much to go on and learn and become part of that Divine Light but had not the slightest notion as to how to do that before we came to help.

It was about a year later that I heard from the woman who had invited us there in the first place. She said that she had done a lot of research on the deaths of those ghosts in the house. She was able to account for all of them at the city hall records division. She thanked me again and again for my help. She had grown so much spiritually from all this and so had her daughter. She was now meditating, going to church, and keeping herself in the Light.

Chapter 18

RABBI ASKS ME TO PERFORM AN EXORCISM

During the winter of 1992 Howie, my ghostbuster partner, got a call from one of the Hassidic Jewish rabbis in Crown Heights, New York. We had met him several years before when the riots had broken out among the Jews and the African-Americans there. Howie and I had gone to this area to help bring peace to these troubled groups. We had arranged for the black priest to meet one of the Jewish leaders and they eventually shook hands and said they would try and learn more about each other so that they could develop more understanding among their people. We saw ourselves as peacemakers. It was amazing that even though these two groups of people lived within five miles of each other, they knew nothing about each other's religions or thoughts. We hoped to change that.

This time, this same Jewish leader called and wanted me to do an exorcism on a couple who lived in that town. He said he would pay my way up there and he would meet me at the train. I never felt comfortable doing an exorcism around perfect strangers so I had asked Howie to go with me. Howie was Jewish; he and I loved to go to the bagel shops in Brooklyn. Our mouths started watering the minute we had made arrangements to go on the trip.

During the next week, we flew to New York and visited my daughter, Sandy who lived in Queens, along with her husband and children. On Sunday morning, the Jewish Rabbi picked us up in his car and delivered us to the apartment building where this couple lived.

We went up an enormous set of stairs and finally reached their door. The Rabbi rang the doorbell and the woman answered. She spoke broken English and graciously invited us into her and her brother's home. They had come from Romania and had lived in this apartment with their parents until both of the parents had died recently. They owned the whole apartment building but only rented out a few of the apartments. They didn't seem to care that the others were empty and had been for years. I suppose you might say that they were very eccentric.

It seemed that an old man in Romania, who felt he could do spells and tell the future, had told them many years before they came to America that they would be hexed and that they would never be happy. Unfortunately, they had listened to him.

I tranced in each of the bedrooms to see if there were any spirits around. Then I gave both of them a life reading so that they would have some guidance. The only spirits I found in the house were the ghosts of the mother and father. They had loved their children so that they had decided to stay right there with them.

We sent them on into the Light, the Rabbi joining us in prayer. After all, their life and duties on this earth were over. They would not only hinder their own spiritual progress by staying behind but they would also get in the way of their son and daughter's spiritual growth.

I asked the Rabbi to help them to integrate into the synagogue. The woman had great sewing ability and could work for charity with her talents. The man could do other things for the synagogue. The Rabbi promised me he would encourage them to get out into society and mingle with others.

They were not hexed nor were they psychologically unfit for society. They had just believed this old man back in Romania and therefore had lived in fear all these years. The Rabbi was somewhat disappointed in the fact that I did not do an exorcism. However, there was no exorcism to be done. These people were fine... and there was nothing to heal that a little help from their friends at the synagogue could not clear up.

I myself was not disappointed with this trip and felt that I did all I could to help these people. I also felt this trip was extremely beneficial not only to them but it was helpful to me in that I was able to learn about someone else's religious beliefs. This always helps one to grow.

Chapter 19

THE GULF WAR SOLDIER'S HOME

During the time of the Gulf War, one of the young men who was serving his country in Iraq, had left his home here in Charleston, also leaving behind an incomplete remodeling job on his home. Just before he left, he had taken down the drywall in several of the rooms and if you have ever been to Charleston, you know that we have a horrible time with palmetto bugs about two inches long and German roaches.

Because the walls were down, the home became infested with roaches and spiders. This was an increased problem since he and his wife had just taken in five children who belonged to her sister. These children came to live with this couple because they had all been sexually abused by the sister's boyfriend. What a shock and a change to bring five children into a home where there was only a couple with their dog before.

The wife, Mona, had called me right after her husband had left for war to ask me to please come and help a ghost to be freed from their home. Each of the children was seeing the spirit of an old woman walking through the house.

I immediately came over and sat down in an attempt to trance and see if I could contact the old woman.

"The priest said he couldn't find a hole to send her back through!" Mona commented.

"Oh, you have already had a priest over here?" I asked.

"Yes, but it didn't help at all. The ghost is still here," she answered in a frustrated voice.

I didn't understand about the "hole" but I continued to try and contact the old woman. As I sat there and prayed, after a short period the old woman started talking through me. She had lived in the house a number of years ago before she died. She wanted to let the family know that they needed to move from this house. The old woman expressed her disappointment that there were so many people in her house. It wasn't that she was mean or anything; she just felt the house was just too small for the family, which had recently increased by five.

I felt the first thing we needed to do was to get rid of the roaches. They were crawling on my legs, which certainly didn't help my trance. I decided to call an exterminator.

"Sir," I said, "would you like to do a good deed for a family whose husband is in the Gulf War? They need an extermination and it would be so kind if you would be able to volunteer your services to this family," I told him.

"Sure, ma'am, I'd love to do a service to this family. I'll send someone over there in about half an hour if the people are gonna be home." <u>These are the real southern people I know!</u>

"They will be waiting and God bless you for doing this," I replied.

Next, our group collected five thousand dollars for them so they could move out of this house and buy another home. When we contacted the spirit of the old woman again, she seemed very pleased. I believe she was really thinking of these wonderful children. We asked God to send her on into the Light and to her peace.

Each year on Thanksgiving Day, this couple calls me and tells me how much they and the children are enjoying their new home. I must say this was a very unusual type of work — a spirit helping to move everyone to a cleaner, nicer place.

Chapter 20

THE HEALING OF A DISTRAUGHT MARRIAGE

In 1993 I was called to a home in North Charleston where the husband and wife were in turmoil over misunderstandings in their marriage. They were on the verge of a divorce. During the midst of all these arguments, they began to see a white mist somewhat like a smoky haze in their bedroom. They were so frightened; however, this brought them closer together emotionally. They needed each other to overcome the fear.

When I began to trance, the woman's dead mother came through and began to apologize for not giving her daughter enough attention while she was alive. She told her that all during Grace's childhood, she was so overwrought with mental illness herself that she did not realize the pain she was bringing to her young daughter.

This trance was very meaningful in that it was so clear that Grace could communicate with her mother through me and they could both talk back and forth. Grace's mother suggested that she attend therapy along with her husband and that they would mend their marriage.

I gave Grace and her husband both a life reading. These readings helped to reveal their talents and their purpose. Grace's husband was good at art and he began to work on his artistic talent. Grace was good at sewing and she began to make beautiful curtains and other accessories for their home.

They had planned on going ahead with a foreclosure on their home; however, I talked them out of that. Grace took a job so that she could help her husband pay off the back mortgage. They were then able to catch up with their payments, start working on a budget and finally work on their intimate relationship, which had been tossed aside amidst all the other problems.

Soon, they were a very happy couple on the way to much spiritual, physical, and spiritual healing.

Chapter 21

MURDERED MOTHER'S SPIRIT RETURNS

I was called by an attorney who wanted me to go to the scene of a horrible murder of a female client of his. It was a bloody mess when we got there. There was blood all over the walls where she had put her hands while her assailant was stabbing her to death. There were piles of blood on the mattress and on the floor where he had literally ripped her insides out.

The lawyer, a few of my friends and some of her relatives gathered there. It had only been a few days after the murder and the lawyer would not let anything be moved until he allowed me to trance and see what really happened.

As soon as I began to trance, it appeared that she had been caught up in a love triangle. She had threatened to expose her love affair to the man's wife. As I began to trance, her spirit shouted through my vocal chords. I could feel her pain as she screamed at her murderer. The screaming and crying took a toll on my body and mind. She kept saying over and over, "You will leave your wife. I will see to it that you leave your wife. I can't stand this any longer. Living like this, being your concubine is a miserable life." And then the complete scene of the murder started revealing itself. He shut her up and he shut her up for good.

Some months later the attorney called and asked me to come again to the house, only this time, the house was empty and had been cleaned and prepared for the new owners. They brought the mattress back that had been in her bedroom. They had stored it outside in the garage.

Again I lay down on the mattress. This time some of her children and other relatives came to say goodbye to her. She was a different spirit altogether. She apologized for living a life of selfishness. She named her children and felt so bad that she had to leave this way. "In my own way, I loved you all more than life; however, I know I didn't show it."

It would be years before I would hear about this whole scenario again. However, one day I got a call from a policemen who wanted me to go back to the house. The new owner's wife had been molested by someone who broke into the house... or at least, that is what she claimed.

I went back to the house and sat down in the room where she said she had been raped by the man. However, I could not pick up anything there. I asked if I could go to her bedroom and trance. There I discovered the spirit of the woman who had been murdered. I also discovered that her own son had killed her. This spirit had been covering up the murder because she loved her son. She had told us she was murdered by her lover, instead of her son, to save him from going to prison.

It also turned out the new owner's wife was lying about being raped. The person I was tuning in to was the dead woman's son. I gave the police a description of the person I saw. One of the woman's closest friends told me that the composite looked identical to her son. He was so ashamed of his mother's actions that he killed her.

The house was sold shortly to someone else. I believe the owner's wife's negativity and her lying had been used to bring me back to that same scene to discover the real killer. When they began to look for the son, he was no where to be found.

I believe there was a message from the murdered woman in this whole thing. It seems that she used the woman and her lie to tell us that she too was lying about her lover. It is strange how the spirit speaks to us sometimes to solve crimes and to make things "right" on this earth.

Chapter 22

FAMOUS PRODUCER'S HOME IS EXORCISED

In June of 1994, I got a call from a famous television producer, Lisa. She said she wanted me to come to New York City to do an exorcism. She explained to me that a spirit of a woman had hurled her down the stairway in her new condo she had recently bought. She had the hand-imprinted bruises to prove it.

I asked her why she called me instead of one of the mediums in Manhattan. She told me that her boss, a talk show host, had heard about my police work and they wanted me to come because they believed I was legitimate. She informed me that a ticket would be waiting at the airport the next day on Monday. They would pay for my expenses while I was there.

I boarded the plane the next day and arrived in Manhattan that afternoon. I went down to see one of my friends at the Palace Theatre, Geri Palladino. She was a beautician at the time for the Broadway play, *Beauty and the Beast*. I had phoned her and asked her to cut my hair. After all, this trip was taken on such a short notice and I wanted to look nice.

That evening about six o'clock, a limousine pulled up at my door and I was off to the apartment on West 87th Street. I rang the doorbell and this beautiful red-haired young woman named Lisa, with a slight look of mischief in her eye, came to the door. A delightful personality and excitement in her voice followed. She hugged me and told me how grateful she was that I had come.

The red carpet in the entranceway immediately conjured a picture in my mind of a bordello. I started to feel the vibrations. The young producer, Lisa, looked at me as if she were keeping a secret. She smiled but said nothing.

Lisa then led me down a set of stairs to an area, which consisted of a living room, small kitchen and a bathroom. I asked her if I could go beyond the kitchen as soon as I went down the stairs. It was a bit more difficult to tune into the place because the cameramen were all over the home. Everywhere I went they were right there recording it. I discovered that there was a long closet-like place right across the hall from the downstairs bathroom. I went into the long dismal closet which was still the same that it was when they built the condo one hundred years before. No one had ever finished it. It could have been a lovely storage place. As soon as I stepped inside it, I felt murder; I felt sick sex. I could see visions of what went on there many years ago. Men were using razors on each other. It seemed they were barbers; but here they came to get some sort of weird satisfaction by tying each other up and cutting each other in different parts of the body.

I could not take anymore of this; so I asked her to take me up to the top floor. As soon as I went into the master bedroom the room changed. It was if I were taken back many years and the room came alive with a seventeen year old girl sitting in the bay window looking outside, hoping and wishing to leave here. She wanted to go home... she did not want to be a part of this bordello any longer. However, she was the madam's prisoner.

I could hear the madam saying to her, "Dry your tears; tomorrow will be better. You are not going anywhere with him. He just wants to use you. You can make a good living here and we will provide you with everything you need. You are safe here."

Then we went down the stairs, the same stairs where the spirit of the madam had taken the producer's arm and whirled her down the stairs, even leaving the dark bruise marks on her arm.

I went back down to the living area on the bottom floor and Lisa lit the fireplace. It was calm and peaceful until all of a sudden, I looked over to an old-fashioned cabinet she had in the kitchen. Here was the spirit of the madam again standing there, making a meal for the girls upstairs.

I sat down and went into a trance. I began to cry. "Oh, my God, a man has been murdered. He has been cut into little pieces. He wanted to take the young girl to be his wife but they got him!"

I suggested that we all sit in a circle and pray. Then I read the Bible that I carried with me. I asked God to take away all unwanted spirits into the Light.

"They do not belong here, Father. Please take them into the Light!" I explained to Lisa that she must help to keep only good spirits in her home by doing good herself. Even a thought can provoke a spirit who has been earthbound clinging to its past. We must all think good thoughts and do good deeds if we wish to keep our homes and our minds free of negative spirits.

The next day the story was aired on a national talk show. The host was very kind to me and Lisa explained to him that I had cleaned her house thoroughly of negative spirits, spirits who had been in that house for many years.

She also explained that just to be on the safe side, she had had a former *New York Times* reporter do some research on the home. He had found that indeed the house had been a bordello and indeed a man had been murdered there. The verification always helps everyone to believe. Even me.

Chapter 23

ADULTERER RETURNS TO ASK FORGIVENESS

One night in the winter of 1994 I got a strange call from a man who didn't live too far from my home, only a few blocks. He said that he and his wife had divorced; his wife had moved out of the house and now he and his girlfriend were living there together. He told me that all sorts of phenomena was happening there and he asked if I would come and check the house out. A few days later, I did indeed visit their small brick home in a modest neighborhood in our town.

They invited me into the house. I had no sooner entered the house and the commode started flushing by itself. The temperature in the hallway was so very cold even though the thermostat read seventy-two degrees. The lights began to turn off and on by themselves. The couple seemed extremely disturbed and stared at me as if they were begging for help. This is so common with the families I visit. They appear to be so helpless. After all, usually before I get there, they have almost always called their doctor, their minister, the police and anyone else who will listen. Most of the time, the answer they get is to see their psychiatrist.

By praying first as always and putting myself into a deep trance, a man started talking through me. He told me to tell the owner of the house that he was sorry he had committed adultery with his wife. He said he was there only to apologize.

Then the owner of the house began to tell me that he and his wife had separated and this young man had moved in with her. The young man went home one night and his father murdered him. After the divorce, the ex-wife was afraid to stay in the house because of the haunting, so the owner took the house back and moved in with his girlfriend.

He said that he had a feeling it was the ghost of his wife's boyfriend but he thanked me so much when I verified everything. I asked the young man to now go on into the Light.

He did and there was no more phenomenon taking place.

About a year later, the owner of the house called me again. He said that he and his girlfriend had gone to Florida for a vacation. He had lost his very special knife with an ivory handle. When he got back they turned his bag inside out to see if it was in there. It was nowhere to be found. However, about an hour later he went to his bedroom to retire for the night. There was the knife in the middle of his bed with a lot of sand around it. He really believes that this knife was brought back from the beach by his ex-wife's dead lover.

"He's still trying to apologize, Elizabeth," he said.

"Maybe he is!" I agreed.

Chapter 24

FIFTY MILLION DOLLAR BUILDING IS EXORCISED

In the spring of 1994, I received a call from a project manager of a 50 million-dollar building. He said that he had heard through the "grapevine" that I had a wonderful reputation as an exorcist. He said he wanted to hire me to do an exorcism of his building. I told him I had never been paid before but that I would love to help him. He said he was willing to pay me whatever I charged because they were losing money by the day. They were already a million-and-a-half-dollars over their budget.

I asked him to explain what was happening so that I could judge for myself according to my own experience, whether this was a real haunting. He explained that the walls were concrete and they had never dried after having large commercial fans on them day and night for eight months. An experienced electrician had been electrocuted while standing on a ladder in one of the hallways, just changing a light fixture. The tiles in the restrooms were coming up faster than the workers could put them down. They had contacted the manufacturers of the concrete, the grout, the tiles; all of these companies had sent experts out and they could not explain what was happening. The doors throughout the building had been painted blood red. Each morning, after repairing and repainting the doors, they would each have big stab marks in them as if someone had taken a knife and stabbed them like a body. The project manager, Mike, said that he had paid an extra 360,000 dollars so far for repairs.

"There has to be an end somewhere. I'll never be able to get another job if I don't clear these things up. I came in here to finish this job because I have an excellent reputation. The other project manager just threw up his hands and left. He was frightened! Please come as soon as possible, Ms. Baron," he cried.

The very next day Howie and I drove to the beautiful building right outside Charleston. Mike, the project manager greeted us and treated us so graciously. He was very nervous; however, he hurriedly led us to the sight of the first problem. Inside the main entrance, which was unbelievably beautiful, there was a huge fan blowing on the cement wall. Water was dripping from the wall, despite the power of the huge commercial fan.

"Can you believe we have been running this fan on this wall for eight months?"

I explained to him that I would have to lay down and ask my guardian angel, Catherine of Siena to come through. I could not explain what was happening until I had gone into a deep trance and allowed her to help us. So I spread a blanket I had brought with me on the beautiful new floor. Catherine came through shortly and explained that the owners of the building had had something to do with the Holocaust. Forty-nine spirits of Jewish people who had been killed in Germany had gathered to make sure this building was not built. They were crying out for revenge. They told us that if the building were built, it would be unsafe for Jews to walk down the streets of Charleston in the future. They were doing everything to prevent the building from being completed. Howie told the spirits through St. Catherine that they needed to go on into the Light. They were living in the past. "God says, Vengeance is mine," he explained to them. Catherine blessed the walls and I finished the trance.

He took us to another part of the building and showed us the blood red doors against the gray concrete walls. "See these stab marks? They were just repaired yesterday," he explained.

"Perhaps someone just wants to vandalize the place," Howie said.

"I'm sorry, I would have thought that too. However, we have a twenty-four-hour security guard system. There is someone here all the time. They would see it if someone came in for that purpose. The place is closed at night and the security man stands right here."

Then he took us into the huge restrooms where the workers went to shower the chemicals off, which they worked with all day. The whole building was just beautiful, including the restrooms. However in each room, an enormous amount of blue tiles were missing on the floor and the walls.

"We had all these experts here. They can't explain it. Here... let me also show you where the electrician died." He took us to a small hallway and we were shown the electric light fixture he was working on when he fell to his death after being hit by a bolt of electricity. I know that this could have been just an accident but it seems so strange that this man had been in the electrical business for many years and he would be killed through a simple job like this. Of course, this may not have anything to do with the haunting."

"I really think this was an accident, Mike," I explained to him. "You are right, this does not have anything to do with the haunting."

I said another prayer for the electrician and ask that his soul rest in the Light and we left the hallway. I explained to him that I may have to come back a number of times. After all forty-nine Jews were an awful lot of spirits to contend with. I also explained to Mike that Catherine was telling me the company that was having him build this building had something to do with the Holocaust.

"No, that is not possible," he explained.

"Go do some research on it and see," I begged, "Catherine is usually right about these things she sees."

Later he told me that he had gone back into the history of the company and indeed the company's history went back to the eighteen hundreds and had been in existence in Germany at the time of World War I and World War II.

The next day the first thing I did was call a priest and a Rabbi. I asked them to pray for these Jews. I asked them if they would like to go to this building with me. However, the priest said that he wasn't qualified to do exorcisms and that if God had given me a gift like this, he would suggest that I use it with ease.

The rabbi said that the forty-nine Jews and I would be in his prayers. They were very nice but offered no help. Of course their prayers were always so welcome.

The next week one of my clients was talking with me after his yearly appointment for a reading.

"Oh, Elizabeth, I forgot to ask you something. I have this customer that I'm losing so much money on and I feel strange about the whole thing. They are building this huge building and I have the contract to provide batteries to them. However, every time I take one (these batteries are the size of an automobile) out there, it suddenly gets turned over and now they are complaining that I am contaminating the property. I will get sued by the Environmental Agency if I'm not careful! I have never had one of these things turn over. There is something very strange going on out there. I get a spooky feeling every time I visit the place," he explained.

"Well, perhaps there is some sort of supernatural force going on there," I answered.

The very next day I had another client come to me. "Elizabeth, I am working at this new plant out west of Charleston, in the part of the building they have completed. They are so cruel to work for. I have had one of the top people call me a racist name; I can't continue to work there," she said.

"Please don't quit there until you have a secure job that you know you can go to," was the advice I offered her.

Two weeks later I got another call from Mike, the project manager. "Ms Baron, you did a wonderful job. The concrete is now dry so we can take the commercial fans down. The stabbing in the doors have stopped. However, I want you to come once more so that we can just clear up anything else. I don't feel that it is all cleaned out just yet. We are still having some problems with the tile on the bathroom floors, etc.

"Sure, I'll come out tonight," I answered.

This time I took my friend, Jim Smyre with me. He meditates a lot and has good vibrations. He has gone to many exorcisms with me and I needed all the good energy I could get.

Most of all, he believes in what I do and that's important when one is doing this kind of work. A non-believer standing on the sideline can really give out a lot of negative vibrations. It can really hamper the success of an exorcism.

I asked Howie to keep Mike, the project manager busy as Jim and I went around to each place in the building where the problems had existed so that we could bless every nook and cranny. I felt more at ease when the Project Manager wasn't right there under my nose. After all, he just wanted these problems to go away. That did not necessarily mean that he believed in what we were doing.

When Jim and I came to the end of the building, we began to hear the rain on the roof. It was powerful! We sat down beside a door, which led to the roof of one of the sides of the building. We opened the door to see how hard the rain was coming down. All of a sudden, we felt a horrible wind. The irony of it all was that it was not coming from outside blowing in. It was coming from inside the building. The door to the outside blew open wide and the wind went outside. I could feel the spirits of the Jews, each personality moving swiftly out the door. It was the most amazing feeling. Jim and I prayed for their souls — that they would go on into the Light of God. We were at peace, knowing that they were now letting go. The poor souls were at last FREE!

Chapter 25

YOUNG MAN HAUNTS HOUSE IN NORTH CHARLESTON

It was the early winter of 1995 before we would be called to do another exorcism. A young woman phoned and said she wanted me to visit her home because all sorts of strange things were happening. She explained that her husband was a musician and he did not believe in the supernatural. He would not be home when we came because he would object to any kind of spiritual exorcise we would be doing. I did not like the sound of this because I always remember the words of some famous person who said: "A house divided cannot stand." It is hard to remove a spirit from a house when any person in the house is not cooperating because he could be the power that is holding the spirit there. I explained this to the young lady; however I did tell her that Jim and I would arrive on Friday night, the evening her husband was out of the home.

Many times I tell my clients, "There is no ghost except the ghost within you." This is very true. Most hauntings come from the fact that there is turmoil being brought on by the people who are living in the dwelling. It always has something to do with them also. One of the great universal laws that I have been taught as a medium is: LIKE ATTRACTS LIKE. We always attract to us others who are like us. An alcoholic will attract an alcoholic or someone else who has some sort of addiction, be it food, obsessive compulsive personality, desire to dominate another, and many others. It seems that the turmoil in the person brings turmoil to the home and that conjures up the troubled spirits; however, sometimes it conjures up good spirits who are there to help the situation, such as this one.

Ruth was only about twenty-five years old and had a two year old little girl who was just darling. I asked her to put the child to bed so that she would not see any part of the exorcism.

It is not always good to expose children to something that cannot truly and wholly be explained to their young minds. Trauma can set in, even at a very young age.

I brought out my Bible and read a passage I randomly turned to. I always get the most beautiful messages this way that almost always have something to do with our dilemma. This time the message was: "Blessed are they who keep their flesh undefiled (pure) for they shall be the temple of God." This was a message from Paul, the great disciple of the Christ. It gave me a clue that someone here in this home was using their body in an immoral way.

Then I lay down and went into a deep trance, praying that God would let the spirit who was haunting the house come through me and give a message for the young lady of the house, Ruth.

"There is a young man who is a musician who went into the spirit realm at a young age, around thirty-five years old. He is a good person and is just trying to get your attention. You are having an affair with someone outside your marriage. You are committing adultery. You are bringing sadness and turmoil to your home. Please, if you want to bring your child up in a home with a father and mother, do not break this commandment: 'Thou shall not commit adultery.' That is all I have to say," and he was gone.

This was a wonderful haunting. This young man had gone into the spirit realm quite suddenly and had been in touch with the Light. He had asked God to allow him to help others here on earth, such as an angel, who provides guidance and advice. There are those out there in the spirit realm who can make those contacts if God feels they are capable of doing that for Him.

The young woman was shocked that the Spirit knew she was cheating on her husband. She was embarrassed. No wonder her husband was not there for this experience... he was not supposed to be. The message and the visit was for her ears only. The young woman thanked us so much and treated me as if she had discovered a beautiful way of life she had known nothing about before. She told us she was going to find a church to attend and said that she would never cheat on her husband again.

These are the kinds of experiences I love to have. It makes me feel so good to be a part of a spirit who wishes to help. Some of us never change until we have had a near-death experience or an experience with a haunting. It can do wonderful things if the medium handles it properly or if the client is a sincere person to begin with... but is just doing some naughty things. Some of us act like children instead of adults and tamper with God's plan for us by thinking that we are just here for ourselves. None of us are here for ourselves. We are here for our mission and believe me, each of us has one. We just don't know it until we start asking and seeking. We are all here to use our talents and our abilities for the Glory of our Creator. We are here to let our Light shine so that we can influence others who are lost in total darkness due to improper upbringing and a lack of religious and spiritual teachings.

Jim and I went to have a bite to eat at a local restaurant and could not wait to get back to my office to pray and to meditate. We both, through our prayers and meditation thanked God for using us as channels for the Holy Spirit to do its work.

Chapter 26

CHURCH ASKS US TO DO AN EXORCISM

In the summer of 1995, we received a call from a pastor of one of the nicer churches in town. He told me that he knew nothing about exorcisms but that he had two teenage boys in his parish who may be possessed. Could I take care of it? His prayers were with me; however, he did not want to join me at their home. He kept explaining to me that this was not his field, that I was the authority on exorcisms and he would really appreciate if I would help him out.

Howie, Jim and I went to the address I was given on the phone by the pastor. It was a small house in a middle class neighborhood. I had been under the impression that this was a faithful churchgoing family. However, after talking to the mother, I found that the father was a drinker and almost never attended church. She only attended when it didn't interfere with her job. The boys were mostly left on their own after school and at other times when their parents were working. One of the boys I will call young Tom, fifteen and another James, sixteen.

I asked the mother if I could spend some time alone with the boys in their room. She agreed that this was needed.

"Come on, you guys, let's go in your room and get down to business," I said with a smile.

Teenagers will tell all if you get them away from their parents and you promise that everything they say is strictly confidential, not to be repeated to their parents. However, one should never break that confidence. They were a couple in their early thirties. The father, a truck driver, was sitting at ease in his big chair in the living room and I could smell the scent of the beer he had just drunk before we rang the doorbell. He had sort of wound down with a few drinks before our visit. You could see that he felt very much entitled to that luxury. After all, he had been driving a truck all day to support his family. A leftover pizza was on the dining room table where they had been eating.

"Want some pizza?" they had asked.

The mother was a waitress in a local restaurant and both of them were extremely polite. They were a typical family struggling to make their mortgage payments each month and to keep their young sons in school. I liked all of them immediately.

Tom, James and I retired to their teenage bedroom and we all sat down on the comfortable twin beds. The room was dark with only one lamp between the two beds. There was a feeling of negativity; I mean a feeling such as I had never felt. It was a feeling of doom and of spirits who were so negative who had taken over the room and perhaps a part of the boys' bodies, minds and spirits.

"I tried to kill the boy next door," James spoke out.

"What, you tried to kill him, why?"

"I don't know. Come outside and I'll show you what happened," he eagerly spoke to me. We went out the bedroom door, through the unkempt kitchen, to the concrete back porch.

"Why don't you guys clean up this mess out here. Negative spirits love all this clutter. Your mother and father work and you have nothing to do but your homework after school. Get out here and clean this up and make it a nice place to sit with your friends. Would you promise me you'll do that this next week?" I begged.

"Yes Ma'am," they both spoke at the same time.

"See that piece of concrete over there at my friend's house? We were all sitting there and I was playing with a dagger and all of a sudden, I tried to kill him with it. The other boys held me back or I would have hurt him. I don't know what got into me. I have lived next door and played with him since I was a little boy," James said sadly.

"What else is going on in this house; is there someone sharing your home with you, like someone renting a room?"

"How do you know that, we didn't tell you that; man, that is cool... just how do you get those things to come out of your mouth. You are a cool lady!"

"Well, it didn't come easy; I was on my death bed when I was five years old. I was dying of cancer. I gave my mouth to God through some ministers who were healers and I was told that through my own healing, I was then blessed with the gift of prophecy. Since that time, I have been able to help others in all sorts of ways. Tell me about the renter."

"Oh, he's sort of cool. He's about twenty-five years old and he needed a room to stay in. Man, if you think we have a mess down here, wait till you see his room. It's a junk pile up there! He plays around with Black Magic and other things; want to see his room? He won't mind if we show it to you," they told me.

I could not believe my eyes when I saw the room. It looked like a cyclone had hit it. It was impossible to see the bed on the floor because clothes, black flags and all sorts of negative reading material were all over it. Porno magazines were everywhere. There was a gloomy sense of confusion and sadness that I felt as I tuned into his vibrations. There was a guitar there among all the other things, an expensive one!

"Who is going to win the World Series?" one of them asked. "Is Michael Jordan coming back to play basketball again? Man, I miss him," Tom asked.

"Come on, you guys, let's go back down to your bedroom. We have work to do," I told them. We rushed down the stairs and soon we were back into their dark bedroom.

"I want you to confess to me about the drugs you are taking. Is it pot or is it Robitussin?"

"It's both!" they answered at the same time.

"Well the first thing we have to do is stop this. Do you know that you have gathered a bunch of spirits in here and they can and do take over your body if you are not protecting yourself," I explained.

"See that picture up there of Jimi Hendrix? One night we were laying in here after our parents went to bed and Jimi became a real person and just got down out of that picture, sat on our bed and told us what you are telling us. He said that drugs were evil and that we should stop this before something bad happened to us. We didn't and then I tried to kill my friend next door," James explained.

"Are you nuts? When you have the spirit of someone like Jimi Hendrix telling you to not take drugs, it looks like that would have helped you to not ever do them again."

I spent another hour with them praying, cleaning out their room spiritually of all negative spirits and asking God to take them on into the Light. They prayed with me and promised not to do any of this stuff again. They promised that they would get involved with their church fellowship teen group.

Then we went out and joined their mother and father.

"I'm sorry but I can't reveal everything to you that we did or talked about, but if the boys keep their promises, then you won't have any other negative happenings in your home. But you all need to go to church together and pray together. There are negative spirits who have been conjured up by some things your sons have done. Talk with your sons about these things; keep in touch with what they are doing and thinking," I said. Have the young man upstairs move because these boys need rooms of their own. At their age, they need their own privacy. They promised they would clean up the debris outside on the back porch. Untidiness should be avoided. It attracts negative and confused spirits," I explained to them.

"Try to be closer to your sons. Keep in touch with them. Take them fishing and spend time with them. Boys are full of mischief and will get into serious trouble at this age if their parents aren't giving them the attention they need. You have two good boys but you aren't paying attention to them. Do not have alcohol or drugs in your house. All of these attract the darkness. Your sons need to talk with you and they will when they are ready but in the meantime, please pray, play and work together," I begged.

They thanked us so much for all that I had done. I felt as if I had made two wonderful young friends of the boys. I heard from the pastor of the church later that the problem had been solved. He thanked me kindly. I would someday like to get with you and see how you did that. However, I have to be careful dealing with a medium myself. But thanks a lot and God bless your work!

"I can teach you how to do this work yourself if you would take the time to come with me on a couple of exorcisms," I said.

"No, I may be kicked out of the church, but thanks, anyway."

Chapter 27

DICKENS AND THE OCTAGON TOWER: EXORCISING MADNESS

"My own mind is perfectly unprejudiced and impressible on the subject of ghosts. I do not in the least pretend that such things cannot be...."

— Charles Dickens

Roosevelt Island is where the big, gray dome (the Octagon Tower) that was once the New York City Lunatic Asylum stood erect ("out on the edges of town, on the East River island, behind stone walls and high hedges") abandoned and boarded-up; surrounded by a fence with "No Trespassing" signs posted everywhere.

Sandy, my daughter, did some research on this building and had discovered that it was declared a landmark. A popular novelist, E.L. Doctorow, had written about (in his novel, *The Waterworks*) the structure having been inspired by Charles Dickens who had visited the Asylum in 1842. Dickens wrote of his admiration for the architecture as well as his painful observations there. That's when I knew Dickens must truly be a great mystic artist of the most unusual kind... that there must have been some other reason for him to have visited the Asylum.

Though he became known as one of the greatest writers of ghost stories and was very fascinated with all things supernatural, Charles Dickens was basically a skeptic. Most of us remember his most famous story of Scrooge – *A Christmas Carol*; but he wrote dozens of other ghost stories inspired by "the grim and the ghoulish through the stories told to him by his nursemaid, a remarkable young woman called Mary Weller, whom he referred to in later life as "Mercy."

Spiritualism interested Dickens a great deal and was very popular during the latter part of his life. He was very skeptical on the topic of contacting the dead and published many articles on the topics of mediums. After his death, Sir Arthur Conan Doyle (the creator of Sherlock Holmes) who was, himself, a dedicated proponent of spiritualism related in an interview September, 1927, that he had spoken with Dickens' spirit at a séance. He had used something similar to a Ouija Board (which I would not recommend the use of). He asked him how he intended to end his unfinished story...

Since Sandy had read about the asylum and then she had actually visited the site the previous 4th of July. She had been curious about it and had had visions of long ago when horrible punishments were inflicted upon the misunderstood mentally ill. We were very curious about Dickens' concern for the asylum and just how he may have picked up on some very deep inspiration there. So while I was visiting her in New York, she asked me to go to the island and pray over the great stone edifice; to perform an exorcism of its negativity.

Upon arrival, we crossed the main street on Roosevelt Island and walked around the outside of the structure where we stood scanning the grounds trying to understand our impressions, picking up on some of the vibrations that lingered. "I'm seeing a woman hanged," was the only thing I said before the prayer and exorcism:

"In the name of the Father, the Son, and the Holy Spirit — Father, we ask you to bless this place and to take all the spirits who are troubled and send them into the Light and into your arms. We ask you to clear this (place) of any people or spirits who have been here who have not been able to go into the Light. Clean the ground and the hospital... and this whole island of all negative spirits. Help each one of those people and lead them into your Light. Catherine of Siena, I ask you to send your friends – the saints and angels – and come yourself to this place and bring all these people into the arms of God. Help them to go in peace. We ask you to help clean this whole area of all negativity, pain and torment. In the name of the Father, the Son and the Holy Spirit, we pray. Amen."

After the prayer, I tuned in again: "These people were piled in there – like maybe twenty beds in one small room. They had no privacy whatsoever and were stripped of any dignity they might have had. How could anyone get well when they had no dignity? There were people hanged by their necks in there; some got out and tried to run away; but didn't have anybody looking out for them – no family to go to."

Then I saw the spirit of a little old woman with long, thinning, straight hair running out of the building down the front stairs wearing a nightgown. But she vanished... and so did the haunting. It is cleansed now for others to move in so no poltergeist or terrors from beyond may harm or hinder.

We later discovered that the big dome circular building called Octagon Tower which served as the administrative center and main entrance hall of the New York City Lunatic Asylum (one of the first institutions of its kind established in this country, opened in 1839), is slowly being stabilized through State grants before rain, wind and sun take their toll; and may one day be renovated to become a gallery or museum. Doctorow, the novelist, is campaigning to ensure that a ruin remains ruined" to preserve the mythology of its original purpose." The Lunatic Asylum was erected in response to the desperate need for proper accommodation of the insane. Previously, these cases had been assigned to a few overcrowded and poorly maintained wards in Bellevue Hospital. In the middle years of the 19th century, the attitude towards the treatment and care of the insane underwent significant and progressive change. Recognition that they required medical assistance, not merely custodial restraint, led to the founding of such institutions (appalling as it may seem) In the early years of the Lunatic Asylum, patients were supervised by inmates from the penitentiary under the direction of a small medical staff!"

Yet I wondered what Dickens was doing there and what he actually saw. I think Dickens knew something he wasn't telling us. The reports confirmed what I had said: the asylum was "plagued" with difficulties, primarily due to overcrowding." The patients' diets were inadequate; diseases were running rampant...

"Charles Dickens was rowed across the East River in an open boat manned by convicts who, as he wrote, "dressed in striped uniforms of black and buff" and "looked like faded tigers." He was taken on a tour of the Asylum where he admired the architecture, (the interior of the rotunda with its spiral staircase) calling the building "handsome" and the Octagon an especially "elegant" feature. But he further noticed some appalling conditions.

"The Octagon needs an angel," stated the president of the New York City Historic District Council. Many envision converting it and its surrounds to a meditative park in honor of those who suffered there. Others propose to build pagodas and dedicate parts of the island across from the United Nations "to remind diplomats from around the world of the need for world peace."

Chapter 28

CONEY ISLAND EXORCISM: THE HAUNTED ROLLER COASTER

In the spring of 1995, Sandy and I were busy working on projects – long distance, as always. In April, I went to New York on business. Before I got there, Sandy had felt compelled to visit Coney Island and actually did go there several times. Like the theatres of Broadway, she sensed a deep karmic connection – as though she'd been there in a past life. But it was sad when she got there — it seemed to be a mere shell of what it once must have been. It looked like it had been bombed and burned and torn apart only to be rebuilt and torn apart again.

When I got to New York, Sandy asked me to visit Coney Island with her to see if I could tune in to its ghosts and maybe even do an exorcism near what we called the "haunted" roller coaster. I hadn't been to Coney Island since I was a young girl so I was excited.

When we arrived, we were shocked at the sight. Everything we'd heard about the formerly great park seemed like fairy tales because it all just looked like a dirty, littered, partially abandoned tourist trap. Like the dying 42nd street of Broadway, its heyday had come and gone and we just wondered what had really happened to the historic amusement park. I sensed the negative, the darkness, the disasters. I knew something was terribly wrong there that just couldn't be explained in words. We walked on the pier where the Hasidim crabbed. Off in the distance of the gray day, a haunting image rose up from the ashes of time; that old, abandoned roller coaster spoke volumes. We approached the blackened charred ruins of what once had been a great amusement ride... very near the abandoned parachute drop. It stood erect in an abandoned field with weeds growing all around. I could still hear its passengers from the past screaming in a mixture of terror and glee — voices on the winds of time from a bygone era. There were dogs that looked like wild wolves from a horror film – gray, unkempt beasts covered in dirty, matted fur, barking and running back and forth as if they were filled with a strange spirit there to protect its fortress. I began the prayers of exorcism:

"In the name of the Father, the Son and the Holy Spirit, we ask you, Father, to bless this whole area... Whatever negative spirits abide here, we ask that this place be filled with love, truth and beauty and that this whole field be used for the glory of thy nature and for the good of mankind. We ask that someone come here and burn this place down and build something very beautiful that is productive; clean all this place up. We ask that any negative spirits that swell in the dogs, we ask that they leave. Catherine, I ask you, as a saint among women, to bless this area and to guide the people to come here and build something beautiful – maybe a playground for children... and we believe that this can be accomplished in the very near future. In the name of the Father, the Son and the Holy Spirit, we pray... Amen!"

It had been rainy, dark and dreary, when after the prayers and rites of the exorcism, the clouds parted as we returned to the Boardwalk. The sun came out and shone brightly. The rain stopped.

I said, "Disney or some similar organization will come here shortly and clean all this up. The dogs are calm now since we cast out all the negative spirits. Shortly before, the wind was blowing so hard that our umbrellas were about to break. Look how pretty it is now!" Indeed, the sea gulls were gathering about the stretch of the beach and the Boardwalk; we felt a sudden peace that was indescribable.

That evening, I tranced for some friends and let my guardian angel, St. Catherine, come through. We all asked for messages.

Sandy asked about what had really happened to Coney Island and her response was:

> "There were three people who were in business on Coney Island, three main men. These men had many arguments and disagreements. They also had a tremendous amount of money that was owed; so, therefore, the arson that took place there... actually eliminated some of the problems. There was much gambling, much organized crime that went on there in the 50's and 60's. There is a negative vibration, like a dark cloud, over that area. It is important to pray for that area. I know the Lord God will take heed to what we have asked today and that you will see some changes there. Continue to pray for that area because it is a good area to bring wonderful things into the city.

She asked if there is a predominating negative force.

> "I would not call it evil, but it certainly is a dark force. Building needs to be continued and clean-up needs to be done because if the people of New York City do not start cleaning up and replacing crime-ridden areas with good and love, there will not be a New York City in a few years."

We watched a documentary that night, which confirmed a lot of what I had said during the exorcism and afterwards in trance. The program began by showing the haunted roller coaster as it appears today, amidst a blanket of fog, scrawled with graffiti. It represents a shadow, and the social decay that Coney Island came to be. The five-mile stretch on the coast of Brooklyn, just nine miles from Manhattan, was the home to three great parks (Steeplechase, Luna Park and Dreamland) which were destroyed by fire (although Steeplechase was rebuilt soon after)... thus, the name, "The City of Fire."

The great builder, McKane, had ruled the island in the later 1800's; but he was not a good man and landed in Sing Sing for election fraud, misuse of public funds and other charges. Ministers and reverends spoke of the violence, lewd sex, gambling and prostitution that went on there; "victims they made drunken and robbed." There were actually three chief men who created the parks and all of them were shady characters who competitively argued amongst each other, always trying to outdo one another. One of them died and another ended up bankrupt. They never really revealed the details of what went on there; but even today, there is an unmistakable dark presence in the remains where the sordid, shoddy amusement shacks still run full blast, where the hiss and boom of the breakers and crumbling paste board dominate the scene. The Wonder Wheel still stands in Astroland. Historians, nonetheless, say we should always consider Coney Island to be "forever an opportunity, a frontier... " not a place to rebuild what once was.

The haunted roller coaster stands as a reminder of years gone by. What's left of Coney Island, 1995-Astroland, the abandoned parachute drop, the Wonder Wheel... remains there to remind us of such frontiers of the American dream. There is no more Steeplechase, no more Luna, no more Dreamland... only a wasteland. Rest assured, though, the place they had called "Sodom by the Sea" has been cleansed. And the clouds parted.

Chapter 29

THERE'S A GHOST IN TIMES SQUARE!

One morning in January 1995 my daughter, Sandy turned on the radio for a few minutes to ease the drudgery of sitting in a traffic jam in mid-town Manhattan. Within that few minutes, she chanced upon an AM news station that announced there was a ghost haunting one of the old abandoned theatres near Times Square. At that time, there were many plans in the works to renovate that part of the Great White Way.

The "Times Square Ghost" had been spotted on several occasions and a number of mediums had been called in to investigate. I was told later that these mediums ran out of the theatres horrified at what they considered to be evil entities lingering in the old, abandoned buildings. When Sandy asked me to tune in, I closed my eyes and pictured the ghost and told her that this particular spirit had something to do with President Franklin Roosevelt. I remember saying that that fact would rule out any other suspects. When they called me, I was able to tell them that it was a kind and loving spirit that was dwelling in the Harris Theatre.

Soon after, arrangements were made for me and two of my friends to come to come to Times Square. So Friday night, February 23rd, we found ourselves in the midst of the haunted theatre at 226 42nd Street. I asked the five people in attendance to sit with me at the foot of the empty stage. We were shown old photographs of the grand opening of the Sam Harris Theatre.

After meditating alone for a while, I announced that it was the spirit of George M. Cohan who was haunting the remains of the grand theatre that now lay in ruins. Its tattered curtains obscured the movie screen, which had been placed in front of it in the days when movies replaced theatre. The dressing rooms backstage were boarded up. The chairs in the auditorium were covered with stains and dirt. Yet it was obvious how beautifully ornate the theatre had once been. The partial remains of a chandelier were left dangling from the ceiling. But the imagery these momentous relics invoked had to be set aside to take care of the business at hand – to assist in what we considered the lost soul of Cohan in completing the unfinished business he had returned to deal with.

The six of us sat in a circle, we quieted ourselves, and I led the group in a prayer to the Universal Source to assist them in being in touch with the spirit. As the group sat quietly holding hands, someone heard the melody of Yankee Doodle Dandy blaring across the stage ... "born on the fourth of July."

Like most Americans, they had, of course, heard the song many times, but had never known its true origins. It was a song that had epitomized Cohan's sprightly, energetic performance style. An immensely popular songwriter of the early century, Cohan had the ability to put into words and music what all of America was subconsciously feeling. He took the old traditional tune from the 1600's and made it his own. He was awarded the Congressional Medal by President Roosevelt for writing *Over There* and *It's a Grand Old Flag*. Cohan complemented his commercial appeal by claiming to be born on the fourth of July, when he was actually born on the 3rd! He even built a large theatre on Broadway with his name over the canopy and decorated it with American flags and other regalia symbolizing his career, and came to be known as the King of Broadway.

The mood was so powerful and intense that my friend Glennis, a young executive from North Carolina who was in attendance, started blurting out messages from some unknown source, "I see an hourglass. Time is running out. We must change our priorities in this country!" The stage manager told us she saw the spirit of a young, blonde-haired woman dressed in a beautiful flowing ball gown from the early 90's. It was magnificent with its gold fabrics and ornamentation.

I could feel George M. Cohan reaching out from the Other Side. I heard him say that Maria (in her past life) had been his wife in the early 1900's. Maria was a beautiful young Italian woman who was the manager of the restoration. She sensed that he was unhappy about the fact that people had not taken an interest in restoring the old theatre. But most of all I sensed his unhappiness with people who were living now who were not as loyal to America as he was.

Interrupted by the noise of the construction and sanitation workers in the area, hurriedly, I asked Maria to get up on the stage and sing to try and bring back the mood of that by-gone era when Cohan was king of the stage. Shy and hesitant, she walked on stage but once she arrived, felt quite comfortable as though she belonged there. I asked her to sing the first song that came to her mind, so she began to sing a song from the musical Grease entitled Sandy and then Maria said, "Sandra Dee." Sandy and I looked at each other as if, we had seen a ghost.

She said, "Sandy, you can make a new start..."

Then she started singing *America, the Beautiful*, "America! America! God shed His grace on thee!" It was haunting and exciting all at once! Suddenly the door slammed and the workers were back. There was not enough time and the mood had been shattered. So we decided it was time to leave. Maria stepped down from the stage as though she were returning to the present after travelling in time. As I started to join the others who were already walking out the lobby door, I had a deep psychic impression of a man in a dark suit. At first he stood to the right of the stage close to the door connected to the only occupied room.

When I started to leave, he turned and walked away sadly saying to himself, "They didn't get the whole message!"

My friends and I returned to our hotel on 7th Avenue where I went into a full trance, with the help of my friend, Howie Comen, to bring through my guardian angel, St. Catherine of Siena. I lay down on the sofa, sang and gave St. Catherine permission to take over my body, mind and spirit to bring forth messages from George M. Cohan. The following is the transcription of that evening's trance session:

Howie: Could you give us the full meaning of what happened tonight, Catherine and what is Cohan trying to tell us?

Catherine: This man is a very high spirit. He was a high spirit when he died. He may have had a very physical side and he may not have had very much patience; however, he had loyalty beyond belief. This person will never reincarnate because he is out there with other angels and can manifest when he wishes. He is an angel with a message (for the modern age).

And we believe this to be his message: It is very important that the people of America, especially in New York City, start looking at their values and priorities and especially at the creative side of themselves.

Catherine: He is not necessarily attached to that building, although he wishes that the building be restored as a legacy to all the artists, such as a landmark to New York City; and he believes that there are people who would be interested in doing just that. He believes the place could be used for talent shows for young talent to help them get started in show business. We would see Disney buying and restoring these buildings later on.

Howie: What about the disasters predicted for New York City. What does George M. Cohan think of the fate of the city?

Catherine: These disasters could be prevented if everyone got the "grand old flag" and did not practice far right wing or far left-wing beliefs but walked harmoniously with truth and love down the middle of the path. Most of all, he wishes you to get in touch with your creative side which could bring nothing but Light to the planet and to America.

We looked out the window of our hotel overlooking Times Square and were amazed that the one hotel we chose, out of all the places we could stay in New York City, was the one opposite the proud statue of George M. Cohan at Duffy Square — the only memorial to any Broadway performer ever erected in the famous district. I looked over at Howie, my close friend and the one private investigator who had worked with me on many hauntings in the past and said, "Well, Howie, we did it again!

"Who're ya gonna call? — Ghostbusters!" That was our private joke.

I flew back home to Charleston. A few days later, Sandy was once again driving over the 59th Street Bridge. It was late in February when she heard my voice over CBS radio telling about how George M. Cohan's ghost is haunting the Sam Harris Theatre. I was telling all of New York City to get back to the good old American values for which Cohan stood. I was speaking to all of New York City, doing just what Mr. Cohan had instructed me to do from the spirit realm. The announcer spoke:

George M. Cohan takes an encore, long after his death. (The WCBS reporter) says the great songwriter and entertainer is haunting the old Sam Harris Theatre off Times Square. "Give My Regard to Broadway" sung by James Cagney begins in the background. The words were so appropriate:

> Give my regards to Broadway
> Remember me to Herald Square.
> Tell all the gang at 42nd Street.
> That I will soon be there.
> Whisper of how I'm yearning
> To mingle with the old-time throng,
> Give my regards to old Broadway
> And say that I'll be there ere long.

... immortalized by Jimmy Cagney, George M. Cohan virtually owned Broadway during the first half of this century and now says medium, Elizabeth Baron, "He's back!" She sensed his spirit during a visit to the abandoned Sam Harris Theatre on 42nd Street.

"This theatre represents all the different theatres here. He wishes that the building be restored as a legacy to all artists such as a landmark to New York City," I responded over the air.

On April 21, 1995, I returned to New York City. Between business appointments, Sandy and I ran through the rain to revisit the Sam Harris Theatre in Times Square.

As I was getting off the bus, I said to the bus driver, "Thank you, Sir."

"Mom, you don't thank the bus driver in Manhattan. Do you want him to have a heart attack? No one thanks another here in this town," she said.

"Well, its about time they started," I said.

We arrived back at the theater. Maria was still there as were all the others whose job it was to rebuild and plan anew to improve the impoverished area. Maria threw her arms around me and welcomed us to the theatre. We again walked through the dark auditorium where Cohan's lively feet had once tapped gracefully across the stage of this theatre named for his good friend and partner, Sam Harris. The balcony was dark and the absent chandeliers hung imaginary and ghost-like above. We smelled it and drank it all in. Maria told us the hauntings had ceased since we had been there and gone. In a trance session, the following evening, St. Catherine reminded us that George M. Cohan need not be exorcised for he is an angel who lingers to help. There is a great difference between a ghost and an angel.

Chapter 30

PHANTOMS OF THE PALACE THEATRE

On October 6, 1995 I visited the Palace Theatre in Times Square. The Palace is the famous Broadway theatre, which opened in 1913 and became the Mecca of "two-a-day" vaudeville. I went to the theatre at the request of some of my clients, many of the cast and crew members of the Disney production currently playing there — *Beauty and the Beast*. During several readings with my clients, the spirit of Judy Garland had tried to come through to communicate messages for her daughter from the spirit world. One client, it turned out, indeed, was a friend of Liza Minelli's and could conceivably relay a message to her from her late mother. Once I arrived, however, what transpired there on the great stage where so many legendary performers had played for eighty-two years, was not exactly what anyone had expected.

Having earlier this year already revealed the "Ghost in Times Square" at the Sam Harris Theatre to be the great George M. Cohan, delivering his message over the radio air waves to all of New York City, I was quickly succeeding as not only an effective exorcist, but also the trance medium through whom Broadway ghosts were using to come through and communicate with those left here.

The Palace was the highest aspiration of so many performers all through the twenties until it floundered to a halt on July 9, 1932 when the last straight vaudeville show played there. Then movies took over as the trunks got dustier, stage doors and johnnies dwindled and backstage lights almost dimmed out forever in the twilight of show business as the old vaudevillians knew it."

When vaudeville faded, the Palace declined and started booking lesser-known talent and barely survived with a "film-and-vaudeville" policy; then, soon after, it was motion pictures only. The Palace's glow died down until, like Sarah Bernhardt before her, Judy Garland brought back the "two-a-day" and revived the Palace resulting in one of the most memorable comebacks in Broadway history. She broke all records. "Since I was a kid, the one thing I've dreamed of was playing the Palace," she tearfully told her audience.

I was led to the Palace Theatre perhaps by the spirit of Judy Garland, maybe by hosts of other spirits who have tried to return to complete unfinished business – to heal the pain of the lives they lived on earth. I can only imagine how let down these show people felt when vaudeville died.

During the trance session on the stage of the theatre my earthly body cried in agony, "There are too many of them!" as if to be in touch with the horrible pain of all those who had been before. I couldn't recognize some of the 103 spirits that appeared behind a gate. We thought their spirits probably remained at the Palace – where they longed to be in life. Once a show person, always a show person; it's in the blood and soul.

I sat down yogi-style and tuned in as the small crowd of bystanders sat in the wings of the majestic stage. All the pain of the many lingering spirits of show business began funneling through the haze of time and lives gone by; and from other dimensions, they thought they would finally be allowed to speak. But I just couldn't stand the pain and it was evident that I couldn't go on too long trying to bring them through. My spirit guide, St. Catherine of Siena, would not allow them to come directly through me.

At first, I saw all the spirits on the stage behind a gate that was holding them back. It looked just like the gates at Coney Island or at any carnival where you wait for your turn to go on the Ferris wheel. Many of these lost souls were so full of pain, worry and unhappiness that might cause my body harm should they all try to come through at once... it would have overwhelmed me. As it was, I could hardly contain myself as I wept uncontrollably. (I was able to watch myself in trance on the videotape later.) I was filled with the cumulative pain of all those lives gone by.

The messages came. Mostly in bits and pieces, I tried to utter them through tears of confusion, having opened myself up to a space too many souls inhabited, stuck there by their own need to finish business which was left undone. I knew no medium on earth could handle that many souls with all their lifetimes of hurt and rejection remembered having dedicated themselves to the stage. It was difficult to understand the significance of these messages at the time; but soon after the session had ended, much of what I said was confirmed to be true by the stage manager and others in the cast and crew, as well as some further investigation.

The first thing I said was something undistinguishable about June Haver, an old movie star.

Then I kept crying out, over and over again, "There are so many of them!" telling us they were standing at a gate or in a cage and that they were all so troubled. It was unbelievable, these big stars who were almost Gods to the common ordinary masses of people on earth. Here in this space they occupied, they realized that they were mere human beings and they could not handle that... after all they had been arrogant egomaniacs; treating their families, children, wives, husband, and fans as if they were kings and queens. However, over there it was different. Their status here on earth did not count. Over there in that stopping off place where we are played back all our acts here on earth, they are common ordinary people who have to answer for the karma they acquired. There, it is pay back time. If they caused pain here, they will experience all that pain over there. And here on this grand stage, it was evident that this was their fate.

"They need your prayers badly," I implored. As the session went on, it was evident that the leading spirit or, rather, the most dominant was that of Bing Crosby. I felt his soul was in tremendous pain over the way he had treated his children in life. He, too, needed prayers to take him into the Light. He said he wanted to get rid of his grief. He said he wanted me to stress how sorry he was for the way he had treated his sons. He had made himself the center of their lives, forced them to watch him perform and mentioned something about a high chair he had put them in as a kind of cruel punishment. He was evidently remembering very telling incidents.

Jimmy Durante came forth and made silly gestures and then told me that Bob Hope would come over soon. I realized this was a personal message for my family later when our own Bob died. And did he give us all hope, leaving enough funds for my daughter to finish graduate school and to make up for some of the things he didn't do while he was alive. We felt the Hope was symbolic. Our Bob died shortly after our visit to the Palace.

I said someone was cursing "Les." Then, specifically, "Lana is cursing Les." Assuming "Spirit" meant Lana Turner, who had recently died, we researched a little about Lana Turner's life and found a book written by her daughter, Cheryl. In this book, she told how her stepfather, Lex Barker, molested her. We believed that since Lana just passed over into the spirit realm recently that this is who she was cursing. Lana was significant, too, since she was Judy Garland's neighbor at one time in Hollywood and they had remained good friends from their youth when they were both MGM contract players and went to school on the studio lot together. Cheryl and Liza Minelli played together often, according to "Detour Hollywood," Cheryl's book. Later, one of the actors at Beauty and the Beast told us that he knew Cheryl and that Cheryl had confirmed that her stepfather Lex Banker had molested her.

Someone who I felt was Houdini appeared in a kind of box stating over and over, "It didn't work." He was trying to get a group together to help his country to be in the Light. (Houdini was born in Budapest, Hungary.) After the trance, the stage manager handed me a photocopy of a Houdini story from a book about ghosts haunting theatres. It was very interesting that he'd brought a copy of the story with him while all at once this message was coming through me. Houdini went on to mention an uncle, father and brother who must not be forgotten. The message, "It didn't work!" is significant because of the mystery surrounding Houdini's death. Some say his death was caused by a rupture after he was taken off-guard by a punch in the stomach as a challenge to his invincible constitution. Some say he'd gone too far with his tricks when he was chained inside a water tank.

Houdini was determined to prove life after death and, though the world gave up on the annual seances, I was happy that I made a slight contact even if it was strictly by accident.

I received a message that there was a girl from another country who performs on that stage at the Palace at night who will be dealing with Hollywood. The spirit warned that it is not right for her. The spirit kept saying, "Hollywood is corrupt. Hollywood is mean and cruel." Then came the message: May 1998... so much destruction.

Later, the stage manager told us that during May of 1988 the Palace was remodeled and there had been a lot of destruction there. The date may have been a little off.

Marilyn Monroe then appeared as a little girl. The spirit revealed that she had been murdered by someone sticking something in her rectum. They said she did not deserve to die — that she was innocent. In spirit, she no longer wanted to be a woman and appeared as a pretty little girl, spreading flowers around to everyone. It is how she prefers to see herself, how she prefers to be. She was holding a sort of Barbie-like doll that looked like her. We knew it was significant that Marilyn's spirit had come when the stage manager told us the story of how Joe Kennedy had taken over the Palace.

Someone sang a song in Japanese — *America*. Some of us who had been involved in Jaco Pastorius's spirit communicating from the afterlife, knew it was probably Jaco reminding us he was still there. He always referred to the success of his CD in Japan; he would come to us and play his moving rendition, called *Amerika* on his bass.

I then saw seven people on the stage — seven who didn't belong there. I saw a train and gunshots. Then I saw a beautiful young woman with long hair trying to reach her mother. I didn't recognize her, but now I think it may be one of the victims of the Long Island Railroad massacre a few years ago. Many times when a medium opens up to the spirit realm, many spirits who are trying to reach their loved ones will come to the medium and try to get a message through.

I was told by spirit at this time that the drowning of Natalie Wood was actually a murder — that she had been pushed overboard.

Generally, I saw very little that was positive there on the Palace Theatre stage. I felt all these spirits are still trying to reach up to a higher dimension and can't get there until they have made it right with their loved ones. They remain because they never went anywhere else; they never grew away from their longings to perform, to be looked up to on this earth-plane. They didn't go on into the Light because they never knew or cared about the Light while they were here on earth. I asked all that were present that day to pray for all lost souls.

There were as many as 103 spirits on the Palace Theatre stage that October day. St. Catherine would not allow any past the gate and I could not recognize a lot of them... there were so many!

Bing Crosby was the dominant spirit; desperate to let everyone know he is sorry for the way he treated his sons. Upon learning this, I tried to reach his sons, Gary and Phillip, only to find that Gary had died of lung cancer only two months prior. According to his agent, some of his last words were filled with the anger he had toward his father and the desire to release it all.

She said to me and I quote, "He told me just before he died, 'I have hated my father for so long for what he did to me and my brothers, that I just need to stop. I need to let it go. It is killing me,' and then he died."

She said that Bing's other son, Phillip, had gone into seclusion; though we'd like to reach him with the messages from his father. They may help him to release his anger and the pain that might have been a factor in his brother's death.

Today, the Palace Theatre is home to Disney's *Beauty and the Beast*. I am told that many of the cast and crew gathered each and every Sunday night after the performances to meditate and pray for the spirits who need their love and parenting that they may one day be released and go into the Light.

Chapter 31

THE BEAUTIFUL GIRL ON I-26

I couldn't write this book without including the story of a very unusual experience my friend Jim Smyre and I had in 1996. I had done a national television show in Atlanta. Actually we went there to tape it so that it could be shown a few months later. It was a show about phony psychics.

Jim and I finished up about six o'clock in the evening and decided to have a wonderful Chinese meal at one of the nicer restaurants in Atlanta. We had a wonderful time after having an exhausting day of waiting around to be filmed by the national television talk show. We both just adore oriental food.

We didn't get to start back to Charleston, our home until about 8:00 o'clock that evening. By the time we got into South Carolina, it was raining. It rained so hard that we almost just stopped and waited for it to clear up. However, both of us were anxious to get home since we had to work the next day.

We finally got to the St.George exit, which is all lit up with bright, bright lights. Just a few blocks before we got there, we were in such a downpour, we could see almost nothing. However, both of us seemed to look over to the right side of the road simultaneously. "Do you see that?" Jim asked.

"Yes, I see that," I answered.

"What is that beautiful girl doing out in the rain?" Jim continued.

"Well, Jim, didn't you notice that her feet were a foot off the ground?" I asked him.

"Yes, I did notice that, come to think of it, " he answered.

"Jim, it's a ghost!" I laughed.

"Oh my good Lord, it is," he said and he was really nervous. He had seen a ghost before but not like this one and this was only his second experience. "Elizabeth, there was no rain on her and even though it was dark, she was smiling and did you see her waving at us. She had on beautiful gray pants and top. She was loudy with that long brown hair," he continued in sort of a really concerned way.

"Maybe she's someone who was killed on this road, who knows?" I answered. Jim shuddered all the way home. This was the big topic of our discussions for many weeks afterward.

Shortly thereafter, a young lady walked into my office and received a life reading from me. After the reading, she asked me about a friend of hers who had had an automobile accident on I-26. She said her car went out of control and landed in a ditch. She was dead when the police got there. Her mother would just love to hear that she was alright over on the "other side."

"Tricia, this is so strange that you would mention her. My friend and I were coming back from Atlanta about six months ago and we saw a young lady on the highway we believed to be a ghost," I told her.

"Was she real pretty with long brown hair and did she have a blue gray outfit on?" she asked.

"Yes, as a matter of fact, that fits her description perfectly," I answered.

"Oh, Ms. Baron, I thank you so much for sharing this with me. Her mother will be so thrilled that you saw her," she said and then we said goodbye.

Chapter 32

ST. JAMES THEATRE: BETTY GRABLE GIVES MESSAGE TO LAUREN BACALL ·

In October of 1996, I visited Manhattan again. One of my agents wanted to see me in action, tuning in to the ghosts of Broadway. We got permission to visit the St. James Theatre where Whoopi Goldberg was starring in a Broadway play. They informed us that we could go on a Monday morning when the theatre was closed.

I can't remember all that attended but I know my friend, Geri Palladino and a young man named Steven was there along with a few others. They provided a blanket to lay down on and all of us went up on the stage. We went through the usual procedure of saying a prayer for protection from allowing negative spirits to take over my body, singing a little song, *Sweet Hour of Prayer* to lift the vibrations of myself, others and even the surroundings. Then I gave Catherine permission to take over my body, mind and spirit and bring through any messages or spirits, which might help those who attended the trance session.

This was one of the only times that we didn't record all the messages, so I will have to say just what I remember that my friends told me.

The only spirit they mentioned was that of Betty Grable. She had a message for Lauren Bacall. She wanted her to know that her acting days were not over. She told her that she would be doing a lot of things in the future as far as acting. Betty told Ms. Bacall that she had more acting ability in her little finger than most of the modern actors had in their whole body.

The other messages were for each individual who attended the trance session. I wondered why Lauren Bacall would get a message, which she was not able to hear. All of a sudden, two of the people there mentioned that they knew her and that they would see that she got the information the spirit of the lovely

Elizabeth Baron

Betty Grable had for her. Perhaps Lauren Bacall just needed that little boost that day, who knows?

Chapter 33

GHOST RETURNS TO CLAIM HIS ASHES

In 1992, I got a call from a famous screenwriter in Hollywood. I cannot reveal her name because she has not given me permission. Her boyfriend had died recently. She wanted a life reading from me. Of course, in the life readings, I do not allow anyone to tell me anything about themselves until after the trance part of the reading is done. That lasts about thirty to forty minutes. Of course, good and legitimate mediums never ask questions of their clients. They are psychic and don't have to. If you go to a psychic or medium and they start asking you any questions, even one, just say to them that they are the one who is psychic and you are there to get information from them, not to give information.

When I began this reading for the screenwriter, her boyfriend was the first person to come through. He was extremely angry that his mother had divided his ashes and given half of them to his girlfriend, Barbara and half of them was put into his grandmother's mausoleum. He was extremely angry that his mother would put his ashes with a grandmother he despised.

"Please get my ashes altogether and put them into the ocean, the Pacific Ocean that I dearly loved," he begged.

I visited Los Angeles soon after this reading and was able to visit with the dead man's mother. She promptly made arrangements to bury his ashes in the ocean. They had a wonderful ceremony on a large boat and took his ashes way out into the ocean and set him free.

The mother and the screenwriter were forever grateful to me for communicating the young man's wishes to them. This whole scenario disproved many things, which I had been told about cremation. I had always read that when one was cremated, they were totally free of their body and could rise into the spirit realm with so much more ease. Of course, this young man was total proof that this is an untrue belief. He begged them to put his physical body back together so that he himself could be free from the earth and go on into the Light.

I suppose some of us are more attached to the physical body than others. I believe that in this life if we continually say, "I am Spirit, I have a body, I have a mind. But the true me is spirit, a divine spark of God," then we will be able to relate and feel comfortable out of our body when we go "over there." Astral travel and out of body experience can be learned which would help to facilitate that feeling of freedom. It would help one to "fly" on to the spirit realm when the body dies. There are many books and tapes on the market on how to learn "astral travel" or "soul travel."

Chapter 34

EXPERIENCE WITH THE GHOST OF MY BELOVED

It is a very different story when a medium such as myself goes to a home to do an exorcism, or sits in a reading and tells a client about their loved ones who have passed than having experiences with one's own relatives.

About four years ago, my ex-husband, Bob Overstolz passed on into the spirit world. Before he died of lymphoma cancer, I had about eight months of time with him after having not seen him for over twenty years.

He loved the fact that I was a medium. One evening while he was visiting me in my home in Charleston, South Carolina, he asked if I could bring his uncle through and let him communicate with him. I told him I would try.

"You know, these people aren't always out there just waiting to talk with the relatives on this side. Many have gone into the Light of God and reincarnated. Some of them who are really spiritual beings don't want to communicate with all the pain down here. They have found Peace," I commented to Bob.

To my surprise, this Uncle Kenny wanted to communicate with his nephew, Bob. Now I know that he was there, waiting to help Bob go over to the other side. Uncle Kenny told him how he had had a terrible relationship with his Aunt Dody and that he had taken another woman into his life to be his mistress. He tried to describe her to him.

"I knew they weren't happy, but I didn't think that Uncle Kenny would cheat on Aunt Dody. Oh, well you learn something new everyday," he said.

Uncle Kenny and Bob were able to carry on a conversation for quite sometime.

And then Bob said to me, "Do you know how fortunate you are that God gave you this gift? You can provide a service very few people in this world could ever do."

"I know, and I don't take it for granted," I answered.

Within eight months, Bob had succumbed to his own fate with lymphoma cancer eating his body away. We went to his funeral, which was amazing. Policemen who he had worked with years ago were there (he was Chief of Police in a Chicago suburb); the Marines were there to honor him for his time in Korea; the firemen were there who he had done volunteer work with. As the police car sounded its siren and went round the bend to return to South Chicago Heights where Bob had served twenty years as Chief of Police, I felt an overwhelming sadness that this moment could never be relived. However, at the same time, through my belief in the afterlife, I was assured that when they started lowering his casket, that a part of this strong and unique human being would live on long after death.

I had been prepared for this death for many, many years. When Bob and I divorced, I had a dream that I could never, ever get out of my mind. I dreamed a dream in two parts. The first part of the dream showed a scene where I was going down an escalator. At the foot of the escalator, I saw his police car. The doors were open and there was all of Bob's blood underneath the car. I picked up the back seat of the car and held on to it.

"Where is he?" I asked.

Someone said, "Oh, they've already taken him to the morgue. He is dead." Then I turned to another dream; there was a calendar with the date, JUNE 25, on it.

Also, my daughter, Theresa, was just a little child when she told me in a reading that her father would come back to me just before he died. Yes, my children are psychic and Theresa will someday take over my practice as a medium.

Sandy, my oldest daughter and I never forgot the dream. She would call me every June 25 and say, "Don't go anywhere, Mom. That dream is a bad dream. Maybe we can prevent the dream from coming true."

Sadly enough, we couldn't prevent it from coming true. It wasn't about me. It was about Bob. Lymphoma cancer drains the body of all its blood and if the blood isn't replaced, the person dies. He refused to take any more blood. He told the doctor to use it for someone who it would help to give them life and then he gave up; thus, the explanation of the blood under the car. The back seat meant that at the time of his death, I would not be married to him and would have no authority over how he was buried or any of his funeral arrangements. Although my daughter, Gretchen was appointed as the Executor of the Estate and I did help her some, Bob made his own funeral arrangements.

He died the night of June 24, 1996, but on June 25, we discovered he had left his children all his insurance, which is how he tried to make up for not being there for them. So the dream June 25 was telling me that something good would come out of that death. The children were able to make peace with their father, which was the greatest blessing of all. So was I.

About a week after I returned to South Carolina from the funeral, I finally had the strength to bring the few things that I was to keep (his belongings) out of the car.

As I was bringing them into my home, I heard him say, "I'm home and I'm a policeman for God." He wanted me to know that so much because he had taken a vow to follow God about two years before he died. It was important to get this message through.

Little Ingrid, Bob's and my seven-year-old granddaughter went to the burial with us. As we were getting ready to finish up after the burial, she walked up to the casket by herself. Her beautiful green cotton floor length dress I had made her for the funeral blew in the wind. Her long brown hair with a green bow to match was a picture in itself to see along with her beautiful little face saying to her grandfather, "Well, Grandpa, I guess this is it. Would you please watch after me and be my guardian angel?"

My last promise to Bob before he died was to pay special attention to Ingrid and Dylan, her cousin, since they were the victims of divorce and didn't have fathers who cared. I have tried to keep that promise everyday.

Just a few weeks later, Bob's spirit appeared at my daughter Sandy's home on Long Island, New York. "Wow, it's a job getting these spirits out of their bodies at the TWA crash. They are frightened and don't know where they are. We have a lot of them over here on the other side already, but there's still a lot to be found and brought over here. I'll be back!" he said and then disappeared.

"Oh, Dad, I'm so happy for you. I am so glad that you are continuing your police work. I know how much you loved it!" Sandy said, very proud of him. She was able to find great comfort and completion by their communication since his death.

Finally after a few weeks, he came and sat on Sandy's sofa. "Will you turn on The History Channel?" he asked her.

"Dad, I have to work; I don't have time to watch TV," she answered.

"Not for you... for me!" he insisted, and lay comfortably down on the sofa just as he had done so often in life.

He comes to me at the strangest times now; when one of our children is having trouble, he's there trying to talk with me and give his advice or comments. One night my grandson Dylan and I were coming home from a movie, Dr. Doolittle. There was a tiger that could talk in the movie.

All of a sudden, the spirit of Bob said, "Show Dylan the picture of me wrestling a tiger when I was a young man."

"Dylan, have you seen the picture of your grandpa wrestling a tiger?" I asked.

"Sure, Grandma. Did Grandpa really wrestle the tiger?" "SURE, HE DID!" I answered.

As Bob grows closer to the Light of God he will get fainter and fainter in his messages and then he will go onto what we know as Heaven and perhaps reincarnate again into our own family, I hope.

One day about a year later, I found that all the smoke detectors in my house started beeping. I asked a young man who was delivering a bed to take them down, so that I could get new batteries. He did. When he lay them down on the chair, they continued to beep. The young man looked frightened. "Oh, that's just my dead husband who was a volunteer fireman giving me a message," I told him.

"Oh, okay, Ms. Baron," he said and smiled as he and his mother knew me and my life as a medium. Then he quietly and somewhat frighteningly left my home.

After the young man left, I noticed the big huge plaque Bob had sent me, along with his Korean metals and other awards just before he died.

The beautiful fireman's award plaque read:

When I am called to duty, God wherever flames may rage, Give me strength to save some life; whatever be its age, help me embrace a little child before its too late or save an older person from the horror of that fate. Enable me to be alert and hear the weakest shout and quickly and effectively to put the fire out. I want to fill my calling and to give the best in me to guard my every neighbor and protect his property and if according to your will I have to lose my life, please bless with your protecting hand, my children and my wife. Amen.

EPILOGUE

Elizabeth Baron has journeyed to where few humans have gone before. Past the stars, galaxies, and constellations where the mythical starship Enterprise traveled. Beyond the Cleyon empires of our minds to what I believe is the reality of death as it relates to human experience.

I have been fortunate enough to be part of that journey. Elizabeth, St. Catherine and I became a team on the investigation of the missing bridge inspector Ralph Terry Griggs in January of 1989. As a private Detective for over twenty-five years I was able to take an inquisitive, defining eye to our journey. As a Jew I was able to bring that particular religious perspective into the mix.

The Baron investigation into spirit has not been a garlic and crystal ball psychic hot line situation. We have constantly delved into religion to help us in our journey for Truth.

I asked for guidance from the Source and I was led to Myrtle Beach for business concerns. My friend Harry Pavillac introduced me to a Hassidic Rabbi from Jerusalem. I went to the Rabbi, told him the whole story of Elizabeth and St. Catherine, figuring they would blow this whole thing off as unholy and throw me out of the Synagogue. Instead they told me that God had put Elizabeth and the spirit of Catherine in my life.

Instead of ending my adventure deep within the archives of Jewish Mysticism I got their blessing to continue. I even was asked to participate in some Jewish religious rituals within my own religion that surprised me. The Rabbi from Jerusalem became my close advisor and friend.

In 1992, Catherine asked me to write the Pope a letter about the sightings of Mary in Medjegoria. I forwarded St. Catherine's meditation tape she had given Elizabeth to His Holiness also. I explained that I was a Jew in a battle against corruption with his St. Catherine's spirit. I really didn't expect a response. The Vatican responded, sent the Pope's blessings, thanked me for my letter and the tape. I then began a correspondence shortly thereafter with the Pope's inter-religious dialogue Secretary.

I have personally associated with clergy from the Jewish, Christian, Buddhist, Muslim, and Hindu faiths trying to discuss what I was learning on a wider scale. As our adventure grew by the years, so did the effectiveness of putting God first prevail.

After many personal contacts with spirits and an expanding understanding of all religions, I have to conclude they do exist. They come in many varieties. Most are tied to our material existence. Some are lost souls. I feel that you enter the spirit place with the same knowledge of God that you had on this side of life. Lost souls who never know God on this side of existence just don't' understand life on the other side either. They carry that confusion into the afterlife. It takes people on this side, through prayers and sometimes exorcisms to help them toward the light of God, so to speak.

Other spirits, called guardian angels, are tied to this world to make it a better place such as St. Catherine, Elizabeth's "alter ego." Catherine, in the fourteenth century in Siena, Italy dedicated her life to serving God, died at 33, and continued to influence worldly matters from beyond.

St. Catherine told me at the beginning of our association that our investigation was not just a missing person investigation. She said it would turn into a major investigation of public corruption from the local level, to the state level and finally to the Federal level. All of that happened. She further told me our work would go a long way to show that there is life after death, that spirits exist, and God exists as well.

The Hassidic Rabbis have told me the way to make things better is to just plant seeds in people's minds. God waters what needs watering.

Imagine, if enough people access Elizabeth's experiences, how many people will not kill or do evil knowing that, just maybe, the dead don't really die, but as Ralph Terry Griggs did, can return to see that justice is done. A whole lot of people would change the way they live if God decides to water the seeds Elizabeth has sown in this book.

— Howard G. Comen,
Private Investigator

CONCLUSION

I have read that over seventy-five percent of all Americans believe in ghosts. There are more people in this world that have had experiences with apparitions than anyone could ever imagine. Many are still afraid to mention to others about their spiritual experiences, for fear of ridicule or of someone just thinking they are not quite all there. However, this way of thinking is gradually dwindling. In other countries around the world, it is considered a great honor when the spirit of a loved one who has passed on makes a visit with an individual; or someone is visited by his guardian angel right at a time when life is very difficult for that individual and he feels he just can't go it alone. In this country, we are beginning to open our eyes to a belief of life after death that had been almost wiped out by certain religious groups and others who are afraid of anything they haven't experienced themselves.

As we begin to open up to a world beyond, our lives will become more meaningful. It is wonderful to know that we live by the law of karma: "Whatever one gives out, surely one must receive back, be it good or bad." Through my experiences with the dead, I have learned that we surely return in a re-birth to take care of those debts we have made in a past life; doing this over and over until we get it right.

There are many souls out there still, after many, sometimes hundreds of years, trying to take care of unfinished business. To name a few, the distressed souls on the battlefield of Gettysburg, Mary Surratt, who cries out that she had nothing to do with the assassination of Lincoln, American Indians at Wounded Knee who were literally slaughtered by the white intruders.

We must, as mediums and compassionate people help with our prayers and meditation to set them free. Anywhere there is a vicious murder or a death of a person who left this earth without apologizing or forgiving someone, there is a ghost lingering, lingering. You too may be able to experience his or her pain or message if you take the time to be still and listen to those calls for help, that help they need to take care of their Unfinished Business. So, if on a lonely foggy night, you experience a ghost of long ago, stop and say a prayer for that lost soul, that soul who still has not learned that he or she is dead. That soul that forever walks among the living until that time when they are set free by some kind Samaritan of the Light.

BIBLIOGRAPHY

Baldwin, Ann B. *Catherine of Siena -- A Biography*. Our Sunday Visitor, Inc., Huntington, IN, 1987.

___________. *Bhagavad-Gita/Mahabharata* by His Divine Grace, A.C. Bhaktivedanta Swami Prabhupada, The Bhaktivedanta Book Trust, NY, 1968.

Bucke, Richard Maurice, M.D. *Cosmic Consciousness*. E.P. Dutton and Company, Inc., New York, 1969.

Burgoyne, Thomas. *The Light of Egypt*. Philosophical Publishing House, San Francisco, CA, 1889.

Cowman, Mrs. Chas. E. *Streams in the Desert*. Cowman Publishing Company, Inc., Los Angeles, 1925.

Gibran, Kahlil. *The Prophet*. Phoenix Press, NY, 1923.

Montgomery, Ruth Shick. *Strangers Among Us -- Enlightened Beings From a World to Come*. Fawcett Crest, New York, 1979.

Raymond of Capua, Blessed. *St. Catherine of Siena*. P.J. Kennedy's & Sons, New York, 1853.

St. Catherine of Siena. *The Dialogue*. (Translation by Suzanne Noffke) Paulist Press, New York, 1980.

St. John of the Cross. *Dark Night of the Soul*. Doubleday, New York, 1959.

Sechrist, Elsie. *DREAMS: Your Magic Mirror with Interpretations of Edgar Cayce*. Cowles Books, New York, 1968.

Spalding, Baird. *Life & Teachings of the Masters of the Far East*. Marina del Rey, CA: DeVorss & Co., 1927.

Swami Papananda. *Genuine Mediumship.*

Swami Prabhavananda. *The Upanishads -- Breath of the Eternal*. The Vedanta Society of Southern California, Hollywood, CA, 1948.

Wing, R.L. *The I Ching Workbook*. Doubleday and Company, Inc., Garden City, NY, 1979.

Yogananda, Parmahansa. *Autobiography of a Yogi*. Self-Realization Publisher, Los Angeles, CA, 1931.

Tanner, Wilda B. The Mystical, Magical, Marvelous World of Dreams. Publisher, Sparrow Hawk Press, 1988

Spalding, Bair, The Life and Teachings of the Masters of the Far East. Publisher, DeVoors Press. 1929

ABOUT THE AUTHOR

Elizabeth Baron offers her God-given techniques for healing, meditation and personal counseling as a valuable professional in the intensely misunderstood, if not fast growing field of the paranormal. In her easy to understand series of audio tapes, she guides the listener through a stimulating group of topics from *How to Meditate* to *Fasting - Natures Universal Cure.*

Drawing on her strong faith in God, she has been able to cure herself of cancer and other serious problems. In addition, she has helped numerous adults and children (including medical doctors as witnessed in her book, *The Art of Silence*) to heal themselves of both mental and physical ailments. Even though her readings are extremely exceptional in their accuracy, she chooses to spend a great deal of her time forming meditation groups across the country. If you are interested in starting a meditation group, please contact New Life Center at 843-762-2123. She lectures to groups about meditation, which she attributes to "saving her life from mental pain." She also conducts meditation classes in her office at *New Life Center.* *"Meditation is more than relaxing; it is learning to get answers for yourself. I would pray that everyone would take the time to learn this valuable art"* she tells her television and radio audiences as well as every client who comes to her. Elizabeth Baron has appeared on national television shows such as *Inside Edition, Geraldo, Crimewatch Tonight, The Other Side,* and *Encounters.* Her radio shows have reached across America and are most informative; people call in and she is able to give them specific psychic messages to help them in their lives. She is also known for her exorcisms, which she performs quite successfully across America. Her current work consists of readings by phone and in person, lecturing through her most popular seminar, *A DAY IN THE LIGHT*, a meditation workshop.

Go to **www.elizabethbaron.com**